The
CHARISMATIC
CHRIST

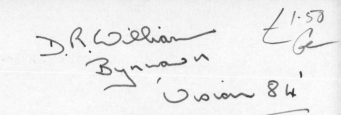

The CHARISMATIC CHRIST

Michael Ramsey

Robert E. Terwilliger

A. M. Allchin

Darton, Longman & Todd
London

First published in Great Britain in 1974 by
Darton, Longman & Todd Ltd.
85 Gloucester Road, London SW7 4SU

ISBN 0 232 51261 2

Published in the U.S.A. and © by
Morehouse-Barlow Co. 1973
Reprinted 1975

Preface

Jesus is "in" — or is it Jesus?

Thousands of young people claim an immediate experience of Jesus. In the midst of this secularized culture they are witnessing to a relationship with a supernatural Savior. They say it is more powerful than drugs; indeed, the decisive cure for addiction. But this movement is counter-culture, counter-church, counter-religious-culture. It rejects both the conservative religious establishment and the radical religious establishment. The Jesus experience is not expected in traditional churches, nor congruous with secularized Christianity.

Simultaneously there has been the rage for *Jesus Christ Superstar*. This weird confection, at once wildly affectionate and blasphemous, has at its center a devastatingly rude questioning about Jesus. Yet many a teen-ager knows the libretto of *Superstar* better than the Gospel. Obviously this situation is media-made — but why this? Why Jesus? From West Germany to Los Angeles people

cannot seem to leave this man alone. Suddenly he
has "charisma."

The Charismatic Christ is the form in which
Jesus is momentarily manifest. He has that power
of instantaneous attraction which is the secular
meaning of "charismatic." But the word is a
Christian word, however much forgotten. It per-
tains to the Holy Spirit, to the gift of the Spirit, and
to the gifts he gives.

The life of Christ is the greatest work of the
Spirit. He is incarnate by the Spirit, commissioned
at his baptism by the Spirit, driven into the wilder-
ness by the Spirit, empowered in his mighty works
by the Spirit, raised from death by the Spirit. In the
community of the Spirit are revealed his awful
dimensions as Christ, not only as private and
personal Lord, but as the God-Man "in whom all
things hold together."

The Charismatic Christ was the theme for the
Third National Conference of Trinity Institute in
January 1972 which was the occasion of these
addresses and sermons.

This conference which had been intended as a
constructive theological occasion became a spon-
taneous religious experience. It seems to have
been a time of the stirring of the Spirit. Echoes of
the moment may be heard in the style of these
addresses. They are recorded without apology
since they may evoke the experience for those
who were present.

The presence of the Archbishop of Canterbury
created a powerful impression. He is, in a mar-
velous way, a true Reverend Father in God. This

comes not only from his venerable appearance, but from his obvious enjoyment of his work as a doctor of the Church. He is a doctor, a teacher, of the Church, in profundity, but also in simplicity. He is not only a prodigiously learned man but a man aware: aware of the modern world, aware of what God is doing and would do in that world. He personifies this neglected vocation of a bishop. For this he is respected, heard, and loved.

Father Allchin has a very special function in Anglicanism. He represents that growing company who are presenting the life of the Orthodox tradition within that communion. He has the wonderful ability to transmute the insights of Eastern Christianity into language and living form for Western Christians. This is particularly necessary now when we need to recover for ourselves in the West the lost perceptions of Orthodoxy about the Christ of the Spirit.

The address and sermon which I gave at the conference preserve something of the extemporaneous form in which they were delivered.

The current frenzy about Jesus may be a fad, though infinitely more than a fad. It discloses an anguished human need for a Redeeming Lord. This need the Christian Church is not now satisfying. People are looking for Christ, and perhaps finding him, without us. Christ exercises a charismatic power in spite of his church. He must now exercise it through his church!

Robert E. Terwilliger
Director of Trinity Institute

CONTENTS

The Archbishop
of
Canterbury:

1. *Who Is This?*

". . .And all the city was stirred, saying, 'Who is this?' " (Matthew 21:10)

We have come here in order to study together the person of Jesus Christ. We do so at an exciting time. The world is darkened by tragedy and frustration. The historic Church is widely dismissed as stuffy and outmoded. Yet the figure of Jesus is stirring many people, especially young people. My text recalls the scene on Palm Sunday when Jesus rode into Jerusalem; the excitement was intense, and we read that the whole city was stirred, saying, "Who is this?" It would be an exaggeration to say of any place in the world today that the *whole city* was stirred by the name of

Jesus. Yet the name of Jesus does stir, and the question in many minds is, "Who is this?"

Well, who is Jesus? We who are priests and ministers of the gospel claim to know the answer, and we teach and preach the orthodox faith in the words of the Bible and the Creed. Week by week and day by day we do this. But it is all too easy for us to be doing it in a kind of vacuum, which does not touch the imagination or the experience of those around us. So it is well that we should pause and listen to the answers given by some of our contemporaries, and start from where the people are. This is the way of the patience of Jesus: to start from where the people are.

So we look around. There are those for whom Jesus is leader in the cause of justice, brotherhood and social revolution. Where men and women are hungry or oppressed, there is Jesus, and to serve them is to serve Jesus and to find him. It is in such encounters with our fellows that we confront God himself and we find that which transcends in the midst of the human scene. So then: into the cities! into the ghettos! into the Third World! Jesus is there. Waste no time on prayer, on contemplation, on liturgy. Go where Jesus is: to the cities, to the ghettos!

We look around again. Here is Jesus known in contemplation, in ecstasy, in celebration. The self deprived of true selfhood by the pressures of its environment reaches out to reality in mystic quest. Eastern religions offer to meet this quest with their techniques of meditation. Drug taking offers to meet this quest in perverted and dangerous ways.

But Jesus meets this quest in an ecstatic exaltation that can defeat the power of drugs and make you different from what you were:

> I don't know how to love him
> What to do or how to move him
> I've been changed yes really changed
> In these past few days when I've seen myself
> I seem like someone else

We look round again. Who is Jesus? Here are people who know him as one filled with the Holy Spirit and as the giver of spiritual gifts. In the earliest days of Christianity there were gifts of the Holy Spirit: exciting, miraculous, unexpected, frightening. So today when Christians speak with tongues and exciting things happen, *there* is the Spirit, *there* the true Jesus. True, St. Paul valued other gifts of the Spirit as well: joy, peace, patience, integrity, wisdom, longsuffering. Yet it is not surprising that people should dwell upon the liveliness, the thrill of the Spirit's actions in the early days and should ask, "Where in our church life is the liveliness, the thrill of the early days?" So here is another of the answers to our question: "Jesus is where miraculous gifts of the Spirit are seen."

So we see three of the ways in which the question about Jesus is being answered. They are not mutually exclusive. But they include two contrasted elements: the neo-militants, whose key word is "participate," and the neo-mystics, whose key word is "celebrate." Both themes have truth, and both themes concern us in our priesthood. It is for us to lead the people to follow and to find Jesus in the service of humanity, in race, in poverty, in hunger, in oppression; and it is for us no less to lead the people to follow and to find in Jesus the other-worldly dimension of a transforming union with God. It has been all too possible for us to acquiesce in an orthodox churchmanship with a flourishing religion which has neither a sensitive social conscience on the one hand nor a lively experience of Jesus and the transforming of lives on the other hand. So we learn from contemporary movements and are humbled by them as we try to preach a Jesus who is greater than any of them, the Jesus who is true God and true man, creator, savior, judge, the way, the truth, the life.

"All the city was stirred, saying 'Who is this?' " Once he is within the city, however, Jesus spends the first four days of Holy Week teaching not directly about himself, but about God, God's kingdom, God's righteousness, God's truth. It is in that context that he would have the people see the questions about himself, his status and his authority. So in these last days there is in the Synoptic Gospels the final teaching about the kingdom, with majestic parables concerning it, and in John the final teaching about the Father's glory. So it is, the true Jesus will lead people beyond Jesus movements, beyond a Jesus cult, beyond Jesus worship, to the Father and to the worship of the triune God. Meanwhile Jesus, leaving the crowds in the city still bewildered about him, unfolds his secrets to the twelve at the supper on the last night.

Tonight in this Eucharist we draw near to Jesus once again and are present at the supper; indeed we are present at the sacrifice of Calvary itself. Jesus has summoned us to be here, so that we may be renewed in our knowledge of him and in our own answer to the question, "Who is this?" We see first the feet washing and then the institution of the Eucharist.

In the feet washing we see three things. First, Jesus is the servant. He gives the example that is to be copied in our mutual service of one another: "If I then the Lord and master have washed your feet you also ought to wash one another's feet, for I have given you an example that you should do to one another as I have done to you." (John 13:14-15) Next, Jesus specifically serves the apostles by washing them; the washing of their dirty feet symbolizes the washing of their lives. Amid the busyness of our service of Jesus and the people, a busyness that goes on ceaselessly, we need to pause to let Jesus serve us, and the service he would give us is to expose in our confession and to wash in his absolution all that is inconsistent with our calling. Finally, the feet washing shows the glory of God, the glory of one who humbles himself in all his approach to man as creator and savior. We are summoned to worship the glory of the humble God. In these three ways the feet washing begins to show us who this Jesus is.

Then follows the institution: body broken, blood poured; the sacrifice of Calvary shared by Christ's disciples to be their food and drink. Here is the secret of Jesus, the secret of the Christian

way, the secret of eternal deity. And when men
and women in the world around us are asking,
"Who is this?" it is for the priests whom Jesus has
ordained to show the answer and to lead the
people to know it and to love it.

2. Jesus and the Spirit

In the bewildering scene in which we are living two things are clear. One is that the institutional Church is under the weather. The other is that the figure of Jesus is arousing new and lively interest. These two phenomena together provide the background to these lectures. The theme of the first is the person of Jesus, the theme of the second is the Church.

You know far more than I do about the contemporary movements in America that are stirred by the name Jesus, and I make no attempt to describe or assess them. It is rather my purpose to discuss with you what should be the criteria for a true knowledge of Jesus in history and faith and action. When the name Jesus erupts in a popular movement, a drama or a work of art, we ask, "Is this the real Jesus?" But equally when we look at the conventional orthodox piety of our own church we have to ask, "Is this the real Jesus?" So, too, our own preaching and teaching invite the same question, "Is it the real Jesus whom we preach?"

There is probably always a difference between Jesus as described in the Gospels, the Creed and the liturgy on the one hand and on the other hand the picture of Jesus that forms itself in the imagination of the devotee. If a Christian is asked, "What do you believe about Jesus?" he may reply in the words of the Bible or the Creed. But if he were to reveal what he really thinks about Jesus, a truthful answer might disclose a picture drawn in part from tradition and in part from his own selective fancy. It is also possible that he might have, despite a sincere devotion to the incarnation and the cross, very little idea at all of Jesus as a person. Then in times of religious revival some pictorial idea of Jesus can grip the imagination and the emotions of many people with thrilling impact. We may find sometimes the contrast between an orthodox Jesus belief, which never fires the imagination in personal terms at all, and a Jesus whose imaginative impact is intense though the image may be less than the Christ of the Creeds, the divine Word who became flesh.

The practical tests may at once occur to us as we begin to approach the question. Is a person's devotion to Jesus ready to learn and to grow? If it is not ready to learn and to grow it may drift into a bog of stagnant emotion. Again, is the devotion to

Jesus accompanied by ethical obedience? To his devotees in any age Jesus says, "Why do you call me Lord, Lord, and do not do the things which I command?" (Luke 6:46)

Our problem is just now illustrated by contemporary presentations of Jesus on the stage. Two instances will be in our minds. One is the musical *Godspell* now being performed both in London and in New York. The basis is the Gospel of St. Matthew, from which a large part of the words are drawn, with only a little modernizing. The medium is, throughout, that of a comedy, overflowing with mirth and gaiety. The parables, which form a large part of the whole, come over with a fun and humor that bring out the point of each with incisive pathos. In the second act we move on to the passion which is touched upon with a reverent simplicity that loses nothing from the comedy framework. The last act is the carrying away of the dead body of Jesus, and though the resurrection is never mentioned the radiant joyfulness at the close suggests that it is a living and contemporary Jesus who is here.

More difficult questions are aroused by *Jesus Christ Superstar*. Here it is one thing to play the records and listen carefully to the music and the lyrics. It is another thing to watch the stage presentation! What is conveyed is not an answer to the question, "Who is Jesus?" but rather a posing of the question itself. His deity is indeed rejected, resurrection seems not to come into mind. Yet Jesus has a kind of unexplained authority which the crudities do not quench. The other

characters are torn and tormented by their relationships to him; what they are making of him is
the problem that recurs. While there is romance
in Mary Magdalene's relation to him there is in
Jesus something that eludes the character of a love
story. She finds in Jesus not just one more man,
but The Man who re-creates her. As to Christianity, the drama comes nearest to it in one particular
insight. While the crudities and blasphemies again
and again repel us, Jesus at one moment speaks of
a power and glory none can understand, the
power and glory of a death:

> Neither you Simon, nor the fifty thousand
> Nor the Romans, nor the Jews, nor Judas nor the
>   Twelve,
> Nor the Priests, nor the Scribes
> Nor doomed Jerusalem itself,
> Understand what power is
> Understand what glory is. . .
> To conquer death you only have to die
> You only have to die.

If *Godspell* shows much of the truth of Jesus
because of itself, it may be fair to say that *Jesus
Christ Superstar* hints at a little of the truth of Jesus
in spite of itself.

Amid this contemporary scene I ask what are
some of the criteria of a true understanding of
Jesus, criteria for the testing of any Jesus movements or Jesus cults, and no less for the testing of
orthodox devotion and of our own presentation
of Jesus in the preaching of the gospel.

(1) Jesus is to be seen in *the four Gospels*. From
them the picture of Jesus is drawn and by them it

must be tested. The method of study known as form criticism reminds us that the Gospels provide not biographies of Jesus or photographic memoirs of his life, but interpretative portraits of him drawn from the traditions handed down in the preaching and teaching of the early Church. So be it. We, therefore, put ourselves to school with each of the evangelical portraits, realizing that while critical study is indispensable for our understanding of the character of each it may also hinder our minds from grasping each as an artistic whole. How different the portraits are! St. Mark in his rapid, breathless narrative shows us the Son of God coming in power with his mighty works, and coming soon to die; and when he dies in darkness and desolation the power of God is there. St. Luke portrays Jesus as the Lord of history with a ministry of compassion for the suffering, the outcasts and the lost, a ministry his Church continues in the interval of history between Pentecost and the Lord's return, a ministry at every stage both down to earth and resounding with heavenly strains of praise and worship, of canticle and hymn. St. Matthew shows us Jesus as the royal Messiah, reigning and legislating, ordering the community he has founded on the rock of Peter's faith, and warning mankind, and not least his own followers, of a final judgment with eternal bliss or eternal loss awaiting them. Finally, there is the Johannine portrait; and it shows us that the cross is glory, that life and judgment begin in the here and now, and that the Word who was made flesh at Bethlehem is the same Word who is at work in all creation.

So those who preach Jesus will again and again put themselves to school with the distinctive Gospel portraits and will ask themselves whether they are being faithful to them. Movements that invoke the name of Jesus may seize upon one fraction or another of the vast mystery of his truth, and we do not doubt that he accepts and uses any who seek him sincerely and draw others to him. However, he came among men to lead them on in the knowledge of himself as a way to be followed with striving and as a truth to be learned with perseverance, and idolatry may be near at hand to those who present Jesus in the aspect that immediately appeals without following him onward in the discipline of his truth.

(2) If we are faithful to the Gospels we shall never see Jesus as himself the goal or the end. He will always lead us beyond himself. In the Synoptic Gospels the concern of Jesus was centered not upon himself but upon the kingdom of God. So in the Fourth Gospel, Jesus does not seek his own glory; it is his mission to glorify the Father, and the Father's glory is his motive and his goal. It is right that any movement which uses Jesus' name should not only be devoted to Jesus but should share in Jesus' own paramount concerns, and it is all too easy to miss this.

Jesus proclaimed the kingdom of God, the divine sovereignty, and he bore witness to it both by his works of power and by his preaching of righteousness. The works of the kingdom of God touched the whole range of human needs, and the righteousness of the kingdom of God touched the whole range of human relationships. So the true devotee of Jesus will always be stretching his imagination to see the human needs and the human obligations that belong to God's kingdom. The hypocrisy for which Jesus denounced the Pharisees severely did not mean insincerity; it meant a sincere devotion to God which was content to wear blinkers about issues of humanity that were near at hand if the Pharisees had eyes to see them. And as Jesus in the Synoptics leads his followers beyond himself to perceive the range and depth of God's kingdom, so Jesus in the Fourth Gospel leads them on to perceive in himself and beyond himself the Father's glory. Jesus does not allow his devotees to rest in the enjoyment of Jesus worship; he leads them on to the worship of the triune God, Father, Son and Spirit. Jesus worship is something less than the worship in spirit and in truth which Jesus came to reveal.

(3) The appeal of Jesus is always *to the whole man,* the imagination, the mind and the will as well as the emotions. Men and women responded to him with the emotions of love and gratitude, but it was his ceaseless concern to let them realize the divine love for them which led them to a sense of sin and a radical repentance. That is paramount. The keynote is not "how lovely Jesus is," but "repent and believe the good news." Not only is the response of the conscience asked for, but the response of the mind too. Not every man is learned, not every man has great intellectual power: but every man confronted by Jesus is challenged to think. It was Jesus' method as a

teacher not to deliver packets of truth all at once complete, but to sow seeds of truth in the minds of his disciples and to let their understanding grow. In parable after parable there recurs the incisive challenge to think. Men are to worship with their minds. No presentation of Jesus is true to him which evades the obligation of thought or seeks to stifle the mind with fundamentalism.

So, too, the appeal of Jesus is not to a man in a vacuum but to a man in the whole context wherein he lives. When a man is converted to Jesus the many relationships that make up his daily existence are converted with him: his role as father or brother or son, as employer or employee, as citizen, householder, neighbor. The man in his totality is converted. Thus the process of true conversion to Jesus includes much use of the imagination about a man's private and public relationships. The whole Jesus calls for the whole man.

(4) The last criterion which I would mention is the supremacy of the cross and the resurrection.

It was and it is sin that crucifies Jesus, and there is no true knowledge of him that does not face this fact. And the cross is both the divine judgment upon man's sin and the focus of divine forgiveness. "His name shall be called Jesus, for he shall save the people from their sins." (Matthew 1:21) There is no other Jesus than this.

In the strange phenomenon of primitive Christianity nothing is more strange than the conviction that the horrible event of the death of Jesus by crucifixion was not ignominy, defeat, disgrace, but good news and the means of salvation. How did this conviction come about? It is true that, according to the Synoptic Gospels, Jesus gave the apostles teaching about the significance of his death. But it seems that up to the time of the crucifixion the apostles had not grasped this teaching or absorbed it. When Jesus died, the secret died with him. Something happened, not only to cause the Church to survive but also to cause the astonishing conviction that the crucifixion was itself good news. Something happened. The apostles said that what happened was that Jesus made himself known to them alive: they saw, they heard, they received the impact of his person upon them, as he gave them not comforting fantasies but challenges to new adventures and understanding. Either the apostles were deluded in their conviction that Jesus was with them again, and their subsequent life and behavior were rooted in delusion, or else it was really true that Jesus had risen.

While the resurrection is thus an attested historical event, nothing is more significant than that the event was the return to the apostles of the Jesus who had died; he was with them as the crucified one, as the Jesus who still bore the wounds of Calvary. While, therefore, I part company with Bultmann in that, unlike him, I believe the resurrection to be a distinct event attested by historical evidence, because apart from the resurrection the subsequent course of events is unaccountable, I am near to Bultmann in viewing faith in the resurrection as an act of acceptance of the lord-

ship of the crucified Jesus. For authentic Christianity it matters supremely that Jesus is alive, Jesus is
Lord, Jesus is to be worshiped as divine. And it
matters no less that Jesus is still the crucified one.
Cross and resurrection, living through dying; here
is the secret of the divine omnipotence. Victorious
sacrifice, life through death, here is the climax of
the mission of Jesus, the true way for man and the
secret of eternal deity:

> Neither you Simon, nor the fifty thousand
> Nor the Romans, nor the Jews, nor Judas nor the
>   Twelve,
> Nor the Priests, nor the Scribes
> Nor doomed Jerusalem itself,
> Understand what power is
> Understand what glory is. . .
> To conquer death you only have to die
> You only have to die.

Here then are some of the criteria of the real
Jesus, criteria for any movement that uses his
name, criteria no less for orthodox churchgoers,
criteria for our own witness as priests of his
Church. But the Apostle warns us: "No one can
say 'Jesus is Lord' except through the Holy Spirit."
(I Cor. 12:3) What then of the role of the Holy
Spirit? Jesus is filled with the Holy Spirit. It is the
gifts of the Holy Spirit that prove authentic presence of Jesus in any age and in any place. This is
what underlies the contemporary phrase "the
Charismatic Christ."

It was by the Holy Spirit that Jesus was con-
ceived in the womb of Mary. The Holy Spirit
came upon him at his Baptism, empowered him

throughout his ministry and enabled him to offer himself as the sacrificial victim without spot (cf.Hebrews 9.14); and it was in virtue of the Spirit of holiness that he was raised from the dead (cf.Romans 1.4). Subsequently the Spirit who flooded the lives of the believers at Pentecost and welded them into one fellowship was the Spirit of Jesus, bestowed by him after his death and exaltation. The presence of the Holy Spirit and his gifts gave to the early Church its supernatural character, its liveliness and its exciting strangeness, the evidence that more than human powers were present.

The images that describe the Spirit in holy scripture are images of a violent kind. The Spirit is like fire, which burns and blazes. The Spirit is like wind, not the gentle voice that breathed o'er Eden but the shattering gale that sweeps all before it and destroys the obstacles it meets. The Spirit is like water, pouring in a deluge that drowns or floods and can transform the hard and barren soil so that it becomes soft and fertile. So it is that we rightly associate the Spirit with the supernatural, lively, exciting, transforming phenomena in Christianity. Throughout the centuries the institutions that represent Christianity can become dull, formal and conventional. But where the Holy Spirit is obeyed nothing is dull or formal or conventional. So sometimes within the historic Church and sometimes beyond its frontiers the pentecostal powers and the pentecostal phenomena appear. Where the *charismata* appear, the Holy Spirit is there; and there, too, is Jesus who bestows the

Spirit without measure, the charismatic Christ.

So be it. But we must be on our guard against a recurring fallacy. It is right to link the Holy Spirit with the supernatural, the novel, the exciting; but it is misleading to identify the Holy Spirit with the miraculous or the emotional. Just as Jesus in his authority as teacher appealed to the conscience, the intellect, the imagination, and the will as well as to the emotions, so, too, the Holy Spirit, who is the power of Jesus in the lives of Christians, appeals to conscience, intellect, imagination and will as well as to the feelings; and he is the giver of quiet ethical judgment, of intellectual integrity, of artistic imagination and ordered moral discipline, as well as of speaking with tongues and the fervor of conversion and ecstasy. We need to turn as a court of reference both to the Johannine discourse of Jesus about the Spirit and to St. Paul's teaching about spiritual gifts.

In the Fourth Gospel the gift of the Spirit to the disciples awaits the glorifying of Jesus in his death and resurrection: "The Spirit was not yet given because Jesus was not yet glorified" (John 7:39). It is after his departure to the Father that the gift is given. In the last discourse at the supper Jesus tells of the future action of the Spirit when he comes. He will be the *comforter* who brings supernatural strength, the divine "comfort" of which prophets and psalmist had spoken, the "comfort" of the people's restoration in the divine favor and the divine righteousness. He will be the *advocate* who pleads the cause of the disciples against the world. He will *convict* the world of the sin involved in the rejection of Jesus, of the righteousness seen in the going of Jesus to the Father in death, of the judgment which the crucifixion brings upon the world and its ruler. He will be the Spirit of *truth*, reminding the disciples of the teaching of Jesus, interpreting its meaning to them and guiding them into all the truth. In all these actions the Spirit will *glorify* Jesus. Just as Jesus glorified the Father in his mission on the soil of Palestine, so the Spirit will glorify Jesus on the soil of the lives of the disciples. All that belongs to Jesus will be honored, received and extended in the lives of Christian believers. Jesus will be theirs, and he will be reflected in them. The test of the Spirit will be the test of what is Christlike. The supreme *charisma* is Jesus himself, in the truth and the character that are his.

Turn now to St. Paul. He expected to see in the Church the exciting gifts of ecstasy and speaking with tongues. These gifts are part of the liveliness, the unpredictability, the more-than-rationality of authentic Christian life. Can we doubt that if St. Paul were here and encountered these phenomena in our contemporary scene he would say, "Yes, the Holy Spirit is here." But it was also St. Paul who taught that the greatest of the Spirit's gifts is love, and that it is the role of the Holy Spirit's gifts to complement one another in the life of the body of Christ, with its immense variety of gifts from tongues and prophecy to teaching and administration. Where exciting *charismata* are seen, there is the Spirit; but where hard work is done with cheerful and unexciting perseverance, where sorrow and pain are borne with quiet fortitude, where scholars pursue the truth with patience, where contemplatives serve us all by praying with a love beyond our own experience, here too is the Holy Spirit, here too is the charismatic Christ. These gifts all belong together, for it is by all of them that the Spirit glorifies Christ. And among the gifts there is the gift of "order," order not in the sense of restriction or regimentation but in the sense of the pattern of a free and disciplined common life. Where confusion is, many gifts of the Spirit may be present; but one gift at least is missing.

In his fascinating book *The Feast of Fools,* Harvey Cox mentions two contrasted types of charismatic movement. He calls them respectively the new mystics and the new militants. Both types are familiar to us. There are those who are recapturing contemplation, the attempt of the self to realize itself in escape from the dominance of environment and in the quest of reality beyond and within. While some who follow this quest turn mistakenly to drugs and others to Eastern mystical techniques, there are those who find in the Jesus experience, the Jesus contemplation, the Jesus ecstasy not a flight from reality but a reality that is God. It is these whom Harvey Cox calls the new mystics. Then there are those who may be indifferent to religious practice and reject prayer, contemplation, cultus and liturgy as outmoded and irrelevant; they express their devotion to Jesus in urgent and sometimes violent social action, looking to Jesus as the revolutionary leader. It is these whom Harvey Cox calls the new militants. To the new mystics the key phrase is "celebrating life"; to the new militants the key phrase is "participating." And, Cox, adds:

> Just as Catholics and Protestants need each other in the Church, so do the celebrators of life today and the seekers of justice tomorrow need each other in the world. Celebration without politics becomes effete and empty. Politics without celebration becomes mean and small. The festive spirit knows how to toast the future, drink the wine, and break the cup. They all belong together."[1]

They all belong together. Let me leave this thought with you. The different experiences of devotion to Jesus — evangelical, liberal, ecstatic, political — all need one another, for while Jesus rejects none who invoke his name he would have all grow in his truth and his obedience. *They all belong together.* So, too, the variety of charismata and charismatic movements need one another, for it is the role of the Holy Spirit to glorify Jesus by the building up of a common life in truth as well as in holiness. *They all belong together.* And while the liveliness of new movements rebukes the traditional churchman, the latter has access to something apart from which the new movements would never exist at all. In the next lecture we shall think of how Jesus intends that his followers will be held together, not by a man-made bond of organization but by the God-given marks of the one, holy, catholic and apostolic Church, whose meaning is life through death. We need to ask

how this Church is related to Jesus, the charismatic
Christ.

3. Jesus and the Church

There is no doubt that impatience with the old Christian institutions is widespread. Too often the churches have appeared to be preoccupied with the technical paraphernalia of religious culture, and to be suggesting a deity who is interested in religion and less interested in the whole range of suffering humanity. Criticism is heightened when churches are complacently involved with a prosperous class structure and seem insensitive to the question mark about worldly privilege that the following of Christ poses. Again, many have felt a want of true liveliness in the Church. There is busyness. There is ceaseless activity. But where, they ask, is enthusiasm or ecstasy or authentic fellowship or passionate witness? Where, again, is the mobility that should penetrate the urban communities in Christ's name? An ordained man cannot but be disturbed by such questionings. I hope I am speaking as a disturbed man to disturbed men.

In America, religion has continued to prosper far into the present century, and prospering religion has gone hand in hand with prospering economy and the security of the American way of life. Now come traumatic experiences. In England religion prospered in the last century among the Victorian middle class, and with us the traumatic experiences started earlier in this century and happened in more gradual stages. So far, you in the United States have seen more than we have seen in England of the intense revivals outside the old institutions: movements of enthusiasm with the Holy Spirit or the person of Jesus as their center. Amid those trends of decline and revival the orthodox Christian can be bewildered. He can entrench himself defensively inside catholic tradition; or he can opt for one or other of the new movements and say hastily that church structures no longer matter, or that because social activism is supremely important therefore prayer and contemplation are outmoded and dispensable. Hence there is an urgent need for us all to have a fresh look at the doctrine of Jesus Christ and the Catholic Church, and to make a fresh appraisal of this article of our holy faith.

As a preliminary to this quest let us glance for a few moments at the ecumenical movement. Here is a movement that in earlier days was hailed as providing the cure of our ecclesiastical diseases, but perhaps it has come to share in the disease itself. I note several phases through which the ecumenical movement has passed.

(1) The first period saw the recovery of the doctrine of the Church and a new concentration of theologians of all traditions upon ecclesiology. I recall the early Faith and Order conferences and reports, the many volumes by scholars expounding the biblical concepts and images about the Church, and the tendency of Anglicans, Orthodox, Lutherans, Reformed and others to vie with one another in showing how good their own doctrine of the Church could be. The rediscovery of the doctrine of the Church seemed to be drawing us together, though some intractable problems were disclosed. This period ran on through Amsterdam, 1948, perhaps until Evanston, 1954.

(2) The second phase, which had meanwhile already begun to appear, saw an awareness that there could be a kind of academic sterility even in the best doctrines concerning the Church, and a sense that it is in *mission* that the Church's essence and unity are to be found. Theologically, this involved a shift from understanding the Church ontologically to understanding the Church as *event.* The Church is to be defined by happenings in which God acts and men respond to him. It was indeed in missionary situations that the most powerful impulses toward unity appeared, and it has been in missionary situations that actual unions of churches have occurred.

(3) Now comes a third phase, perhaps the most confused but perhaps the one which may prove to be the most creative. This phase was apparent at

New Delhi in 1961, in the Second Vatican Council from 1962 onward and in much that has happened since.

What are the marks of this third phase? There is the emphasis upon renewal as the clue to unity. Renewal means that the question shifts from "How can we unite our existing church structures?" "How can we reconcile our existing traditions?" to "How may our churches be renewed and reformed so as to be more obedient to Christ in their form, their behavior, their mission?" and "What can we learn from one another in this process?" The vision of Pope John XXIII did much to set renewal and reform at the heart of the ecumenical quest.

Besides renewal, a mark of this phase is the belief that we understand the Church not by concentrating on it as a thing-in-itself but by looking beyond the Church to the world it exists to serve and to re-create. To illustrate my meaning let me quote from a World Council of Churches publication, *The Church for Others.*

> The Church exists for the world. . . the Church lives in order that the world may know its own true being. It is *pars pro toto;* it is the firstfruits of the new creation. . . its centre lies outside itself; it must live 'ex-centredly'. It has to seek out those situations in the world which call for loving responsibility, and there it must convince and point to *Shalom.*"[2]

The same theme is found in the writings of the Roman Catholic theologian Hans Urs von Balthasar. In his book, *A Theology of History,*[3] he argues that the Church is the servant of God's purpose in and for history, and for that reason must not look for history to be drawn into itself. The Church, he says, is sent into the world to be itself a picture of the world becoming re-created after God's will. With this way of thinking about the Church's role there is linked the social activism prominent in the ecumenical movement at this time, a social activism seen for instance at Uppsala in 1968 with the concern about race, poverty, pollution and the Third World. But it would be a mistake to see only left wing activism in this phase. It goes deeper. The concept of "the Church for the world" is akin to the ancient Greek theology which teaches that through the existence of the Church as the body of the risen Jesus Christ the world itself begins to be re-created.[4]

It is in the context of the "Church for the world" theme that we frequently hear the church described as the servant. No longer does the Church enjoy the position of cultural dominance it once enjoyed in Western society. It needs to be more aware of this than it sometimes realizes, and to be less ready to use the world's privileges as its props. But the servant concept divides into a superficial notion, which is all too prominent, and a deeper notion, which is theologically based. It is not for the Church to serve the world by offering the world solutions to its problems as the world itself sees them. Rather does the Church serve the world by teaching it unpalatable truths and witnessing to its need for re-creation. But the true and positive meaning of the servant concept is that the Church tries not just to draw people within its own religious activities, but to enter the situations in which people live and try to transform some of the world's behavior into Christian behavior.

This last phase of the ecumenical movement, with the emphasis upon renewal and upon the world's re-creation, has had this result: There is now far less interest than there used to be in ecclesiastical structures and in "reunion" as it was commonly understood. C.O.C.U. in the United States and the similar reunion projects in other countries are arousing far less interest today. This may be due partly to a timid drawing back from commitment, but it is partly because such reunion schemes no longer seem to have the first priority. The recent trends cause churchmen often to be more interested in what they may be doing together, here and now, in mission and in the service of humanity. And there is the further point that problems about uniting the institutions are less in mind than the prior problem of the institution itself.

So we turn to the question of the institution and the life of the Spirit. How are they related?

The contemporary scene is filled by many revival movements: the pentecostal churches, the Jesus movements, the various militant groups of Christian activism. The Spirit blows where he wills; and blow he does, in ecstasy, in fellowship, in Jesus witness, in social action. Harvey Cox has well described the problem that arises. In *The Secular City* he wrote:

> The real ecumenical crisis today is not between Catholics and Protestants, but between traditional and experimental forms of Church life." And he added: "If Church leaders do not recognize this, within a few decades we shall see a cleavage in the Church that will be comparable to the one that appeared in the sixteenth century.[5]

The cleavage is already with us. Some Christians are on one side or the other of the divide. Others are torn within themselves between a loving loyalty to the deep treasures of the past and a sensitivity to what is lively in the contemporary scene. It is, therefore, urgent for us to explore again the doctrine concerning the Christ, the Spirit and the Catholic Church.

In making this reappraisal we turn to the New Testament for our authority. But we need to pay more attention to the presence within the New Testament writings of a kind of double polarity — the historical givenness of the Church on the one hand and the recurring creative energies of the Holy Spirit on the other.

The Messiah implies the messianic community, and from the midst of an Israel that was rejecting him Jesus gathered a remnant to be the nucleus of a new Israel and trained them to be his people with whom he made a new covenant in his death. The new *ecclesia* was under the continuing lordship of the risen Jesus and was indwelt by his

Spirit, its members called to be saints. In order to be faithful to the lordship of Jesus in truth and in life the Church needed both a tradition of rite and teaching that witnessed to Christ's words and acts in history and also an openness to the actions of the Holy Spirit in particular situations, challenging, interpreting, commanding. These two aspects of the Church's essential life are sometimes called the horizontal and the vertical, and both are necessary. If it relied on the vertical action of the Holy Spirit alone, the Church might be misled through forgetting the total stream of Christian experience and the basic truth of Christ once revealed in history. But if it relied on the horizontal tradition alone, the Church could let its hold upon basic truth become fossilized through missing the Spirit's challenges to new perceptions and new actions. It is not difficult to see in past history the interplay of these two factors. When the Church faced the challenge of Gnosticism in the second century, there was urgent need for the horizontal traditions of scripture and apostolic succession to conserve the essence of Christianity. When however the medieval church grew stagnant and corrupt, the vertical was needed with the explosive dynamism of the Reformers. In England when the Church was in danger of losing its credentials early in the nineteenth century, there came the Tractarian recovery of the horizontal truth of "our apostolic descent"; but subsequently it was a false horizontalism, which tried to resist the new understanding of revelation brought by the historical and biological sciences.

The tradition is indeed God-given and Christ-made. It is not for the Church to abandon the scriptures or the sacraments or the apostolic ministry. In the first book I ever wrote, as a very young man, *The Gospel and the Catholic Church* (1936) I advanced the thesis that the Church's visible order is the expression of the gospel in its historical givenness; and that, by the dying to self of the members in union with one another and with Christ, the structure of the Church witnesses to Christ's death and resurrection. "The structure of Catholicism," I wrote, "is the expression of the Gospel." If you ask me whether today, after thirty-six years, I still adhere to this youthful thesis, my answer is, Yes, I adhere to it. But I note one difference. I would not now press the metaphor of *structure* in the same way, for the language of structure is but one among several metaphors for the Church, and all the metaphors need to be seen together: temple, body, vine, *ecclesia*. Each of the metaphors speaks of the once-for-all givenness of the Church; and each of them also speaks of continuous growth. Into the metaphor of the temple, for instance, which might seem of itself to be static, there bursts another metaphor, for the stones of the temple are *living* stones, belying a static rigidity. So the sacramental order of the Church witnesses to its historical givenness and witnesses also to its growth toward a future plenitude when, partly within history and partly beyond history, the Church will become perfectly what it is already.

In a striking essay in his book *Chrétiens en*

Dialogue,[6] Father Yves Congar showed how the thought of the Church as once for all created and as also growing to a future plenitude can help in the combining of a Catholic ecclesiology with a recognition of the spiritual significance of communities outside the Catholic Church. He suggested that movements outside the historic institution may help to correct the institution's failings and may contribute to the Church's growth into the full understanding of itself. He went on to depict the final unity not as a process of those outside "coming back to Mother" but as the converging of all Christian communities upon a goal that will be in continuity with the Church's historic past. Father Congar traced his thesis in relation to Rome and the churches outside the Roman Communion. May we apply the same principle to our own problems of the institutional Church in relation to the charismatic movements? While we may not see all the answers, we may at least see our way forward on his lines. We cherish the historic norms of catholicity in scripture, creed, sacrament and apostolic succession; but we cherish them not as the walls of an enclosed fortress but as gifts of God for the building up of the Church in unity and in truth. While God bids us be faithful to these gifts, he who was able to raise up children to Abraham from the stones of the Judean desert is able to use for the ends of his Church even the strangest of movements in the contemporary scene. So we are called to cherish the horizontal tradition that reaches across the centuries of history and also to be alert to the vertical actions of the Holy Spirit here and now. To do this is a difficult adventure, and we may fail to find a logical synthesis of what we are doing. But it is not an adventure that can imperil our souls. No, our souls would be imperiled if we were content either to rest within a static structure of tradition or to be swept into some enthusiastic movement of the day, without relating it to the larger world of catholic truth and life.

Amid these tensions in the world and in the Church the strains that come to a priest are formidable, and there have been those who have broken under these strains. I believe however that the historic role of the priest still stands, however changed its outward garb and context may have become.

The priest is still the *preacher and teacher*. While he may often carry out this role in informal ways rather than by pulpit oratory, the role continues. As teacher he draws out of his treasure things new and old; he alerts the people to new spiritual movements and to the new tasks of social action and witness, and in so doing he draws upon the old, timeless doctrines of God, Christ and Man. It is a role more arduous and more exciting than perhaps ever in the past.

The priest is still the *absolver*. Amid the clinical trends in contemporary pastoral guidance he will keep alive the permanent issues of sin and forgiveness. To be healthy and to be whole is no substitute for being penitent, forgiven and holy. The priest's own frequent penitence will be a sure foundation. But in the ministry of reconciliation he finds himself increasingly concerned not only with the absolving of individuals but with the reconciling of persons and groups to one another, and the illustrations of this are legion.

The priest is *prophet*. He may not possess a special charisma of prophecy, and he will not pretend to gifts he does not have. There are sometimes men and women among the laity who have great prophetic gifts. But no priest is without the prophetic responsibility of using the imagination in seeing and showing the implications of Christian belief. It is here that the priest will be striving not only to bring people inside the Church's life but to bring the Church's witness inside the social situations in the cities.

The priest is still the *man of prayer*. The trends away from devotion and cultus are intelligible enough, as we learn that the world is God's and our service of God is always in it and through it. But prayer and worship are the supreme privileges of the creature and child of God created in God's own image, and to belittle them is to be unfaithful to Christ. Amid the spiritual hunger of our times, when many, whose souls are starved by activism, are seeking guidance in the contemplation of God, a terrible judgment rests upon the priest who is unable to give help or guidance because he has ceased to be a man of prayer himself.

The priest is the *man of the Eucharist*. In his role as celebrant he represents not only the congregation locally present but Christ and the whole Church across the ages. The vertical and the horizontal are here supremely blended, for the

Eucharist is the blending in Christ of the past, the present and the future.

Was there ever a more exciting time in which to be a priest in the Church of God? It is our office to cherish the deep things of tradition and to be bold in experiment, to lead the people in the arts of prayer and contemplation and into the service of the world's re-creation, to let our hearts be broken by the world's suffering and filled with the joy of Christ.

I end by asking you to consider how the Eucharist sums up the relation between Christ, the Church and the world.

Recall the scene of the institution. The Lord Jesus is with the apostles on the last night. They are celebrating — celebrating as at every Passover time the goodness of the God who had led them out of slavery in Egypt many centuries ago, and celebrating the hope of heaven and of good things to come. The sad and somber setting of imminent death for Jesus and an unknown future for the disciples does not dim the joy of celebrating. And now the Lord speaks: "This is my body, given for you"; "This is my blood of the covenant, shed for you." Body broken, blood poured: it means Jesus himself, Jesus in his death. On the next day he is going to die; and the death on a mound outside the city gate will be an event outside them, an event to watch perhaps from near or perhaps from a distance, but an event outside them. But eat! drink! The death is to become not only outside them, but within them; it will be their food and their drink, the stuff of

their own lives. It will be within, part of them.
Some years later we hear the apostle Paul saying to
the Christians of Corinth: "The cup which we
drink, is it not a sharing in the blood of Christ? the
loaf which we eat, is it not a sharing in the body of
Christ?" (I Cor. 10:16) So in the Eucharist the Lord
draws the people to share in his own living-
through-dying.

While the Eucharist draws us from the world to
share in Christ's sacrifice together with the whole
company of heaven, it also draws us to share in
Christ's outgoing action toward the world for the
world's re-creation. If we receive the sacrament
upon our knees nothing more befits the reverence and the adoration in our hearts. But if we
receive the sacrament standing, as was probably
the custom in the early Church, nothing more
befits our attitude of obedience as men and
women ready to go out, to act and to do. For Jesus
who is the Word of the Father feeds us so that we
may share increasingly with him in the world's re-
creation. He does not feed us in order to draw us
away with him into a separated realm of religion,
but in order to draw us into participation with him
in his work of molding the world into his own
likeness.

This aspect of the Eucharist was powerfully
drawn out by Dr. Arthur Vogel, formerly Professor
of Dogmatic Theology at Nashotah House and
now Bishop of West Missouri, in his book *Is the
Last Supper Finished?*:[7]

For Christians, the creation of God's world is still

going on through men, and Providence is the name of the process.

The Christians' liturgy is to continue God's creation of the world through their incorporation into his Body-Word Jesus Christ. In God's community his people receive his meaning (his Word) in order to manifest their meaning through their bodily lives wherever they are in the universe.

If the nature of the Eucharist is as I have described it, narrow provincialism of any kind is impossible in Christian living. We cannot participate in Christ's self-giving death through the eucharistic liturgy and then try to protect ourselves by his food. In the mystical and sacramental bodies of Christ, God is among us still doing his work in creating the world.

Through the Eucharist we are extensions of Christ's vulnerability, sustained by the food of his victory; we are not guards placed at the door of his ante-room to protect him from profanation or contact with the world.

One last quotation, to excite your interest in Dr. Vogel's book if you do not already know it:

> The Word of God cannot be read or heard as if it were past, abstract, finished or something to be used by us. By rejoicing in it we give ourselves so completely to it that we in one sense become it; to the extent that we become it we are its proclamation."[8]

Thus the blessed sacrament sustains us so that we are ourselves Christ's body in the re-creation of the world. In the sacrament we are one with the risen Jesus, one with the saints in heaven, the mother of the Lord and the holy angels; but as love is one and indivisible the Eucharist is the gate of heaven only as being also the gate through which we go out in the service of the world. In the sacrament the antinomies of which we have been thinking are united and the fragmentary insights and apprehensions of Christians are joined in one. Here the new militant is given the humility with which alone his warfare will be Christian, the activist is called to silence for a space to contemplate his savior, the new mystic is shown the true goal of his quest, and all of us celebrate the sorrow and the joy of Jesus in the glory of the triune God. So the Eucharist sums up the relation of God, Christ and the world.

Robert E. Terwilliger

4. The Charismatic Christ and Christian Theology

In the 1970's Christians are entering a new era. In the midst of considerable turbulence, a repossession of faith is emerging. The theological revolution of the 60's seems curiously dated, yet to understand what is now going on, it is necessary to remember what happened during the past decade.

Let us begin, perhaps not too arbitrarily, with the year 1963, when the little book called *Honest to God* was published. It was recently said that the book now looks like a period piece. Its author, John Robinson, Bishop of Woolwich, had previously made a good name in biblical scholarship. He diverted from his specialty and undertook to express his views on the need for a radical re-conception of the Christian image of God. Neither he nor his publisher regarded this essay as a book of moment. It proved an astonishing, crazy success. It sold an incredible number of copies and started something of a theological movement in the Anglo-Saxon world and beyond.

To look at this book now and realize its history is a matter of amazement. Superficially it seems to be an act of disinterment. The figures spotlighted in the discussion — Tillich, Bultmann, Bonhoeffer — were venerable if not dead. Those of us who had received an earlier theological education in America seemed to be reliving a previous experience or existence because these men belong to the era of the 30's, the 40's and the 50's. But the confection Bishop Robinson made by sloganizing certain elements in their writings was a catalyst. Jesus as "the man for others"; modern man "come of age"; God as "Ground of Being" rather than "up there" or "out there" — these catch words passed instantly into the jargon of a new, exciting religious conversation.

It seemed as though we had entered into a new era of Christianity, the era of the inevitable future, which would be radically in contradiction to the experience theologically and spiritually of previous decades and, indeed, of centuries. A kind of watered down neo-orthodoxy dominated the ecumenical scene; it had become a kind of Protestant consensus. We began to be bored with Barth; in fact, we were tempted to be bored with the Word of God since Barth was the prophet of the Word of God. Of course, we had forgotten what

Barth really said, and what Brunner and the brothers Niebuhr had said, but we did not need such a radical conception of man's need and such a radical hope for God's initiative as we did in the time of tragedy, of depression and war. We were economically in a state of considerable prosperity, and the wars we were fighting were rather far away. So it was a time for an optimistic man-centered theology, a theology of relative prosperity and peace. This mood was very similar to the mind of the 1920's when similar secular conditions prevailed. *Honest to God* crystalized something of this temper. Here was a new focus on man and his potential, even with a strong suggestion that he could pretty well go it alone. Here was a rejection of transcendence and a vivid reaffirmation of the immanence of God.

This book signaled the beginning of a new kind of theological writing. It was "pop theology." It marked the beginning of the change in locus of theological discussion. No longer was talk of God confined to theological journals, seminaries and pulpits; it was cocktail party conversation. For a period of time there was a great burst of religious publishing. Religion became one of the most popular forms of nonfiction. Theological writing was journalistic. It also shared the problems of journalism because what is newsworthy is what is uncharacteristic.

The theological freak, the theologian who believed God was dead, the bishop who did not believe in the Trinity got the attention as we entered into a period of increasing negativism.

Everyone was talking about God, but not many seemed to be believing in him.

Religion, having become newsworthy, became media-made. It is reported that the "death of God theologians" did not know they were a school until they read about it in *Time* magazine. Whether this delightful gossip is true or not, there was the beginning of an era of rapid fads, a sure mark of the media-made mind — *Honest to God,* "death of God," *The Secular City,* followed by a variety of lesser fashions. These fads were "in" for a period of only two or three years before they were superseded. They were characterized by a proliferation of slogans which had almost the power of television commercials. A new kind of religious celebrity emerged, such as Bishop Pike and Harvey Cox, who personified these passing moods. In this turbulence, religion became an area of insecurity and flux rather than a source of assurance.

The new Roman Catholicism that emerged after Vatican II influenced us all far more than we have ever really sensed. No longer did we have the great monolithic, assured, substantial Rome which had occupied the position of "father figure." It had always been there, available to aggress against, available to define oneself against. In fact, it began to be difficult to be a Protestant because there was less and less to protest against. Within the Roman Catholic Church there developed an instability far greater than we expected. Not only were Papal authority and the birth control ethic being questioned but the very reality of the supernatural itself. We have all felt the tremor caused by the fall of Rome's sense of certainty, of its confident catholic and Christian identity.

A growing threatening fear increased among churchmen, particularly among clerics. It is a terrifying thought to a man who wears a round collar that the future of man might be non-religious. Was what Bonhoeffer said really true in those last enigmatic writings he penned in prison? Was it true that in the future we must learn to speak in a secular fashion about God? To live before God as if there were no God? Was it true that in the future religion would be gradually, or perhaps suddenly, outgrown? Was it true indeed that one of the vocations of Christians was to produce a nonreligious, secularized gospel? Would Christianity become something it never was before? Was this true?

We came increasingly to believe that all this was true. Even our religious establishments, our various Vaticans, came to believe that it was true. They have been operating, more or less, on this assumption ever since.

This assumption is not true: It has been discredited not by theologians, but by events. In fact, we were entering — not a secularized age, as we thought — we were entering then an age of incredible religiosity. "Modern man cannot believe in" is one of the most fatuous phrases we have been gullible enough to accept. Modern man is quite capable of believing in anything, and is doing it. At the very time churchmen were deceiving themselves about the nonreligious future, the American people were beginning a new quest for the supernatural with the Maharishi Mahesh Yogi, the novels of Herman Hesse, spiritualism, and psychedelic drugs. For the vulgar there was astrology — the new established religion. Modern man has a terrible need for a satisfaction of spiritual hunger that the materialistic technological culture we have created cannot satisfy.

This very clearly is a call to the Church. It is not a call to return to the old things, but rather to realize that a new miracle of the Spirit is necessary to produce religion that is adequate for modern man. We were wondering what this miracle might be.

Suddenly people began to be interested in Jesus. This also was not supposed to be. For some years we had been rather embarrassed with Jesus; we had assumed that it was impossible for a twentieth century man to relate to this first century man. Furthermore, we were being told that the Gospels are so full of an outmoded world view that they are almost impossible to use. Jesus might be accepted as one of the "Christ figures" of history, but remarkably unknowable through the Gospels, surely unmiraculous, devastatingly culturally conditioned. This Jesus might be the Christ of our choice but there was nothing about him that was final, nothing saving.

But suddenly people began to be interested in Jesus. This was not simply the beautiful man and ideal teacher, this was the Jesus of gospel, the Jesus of saving, supernatural power, of the "Jesus movement." Such a development was significant because it meant a change from thinking of God in general to thinking of God in particular. So long as we considered God as "ground of being" and in other vague and generalized terms of immanence, the question of God remained very much under our own control. We were not very much threatened by the ground of being coming upon us in sudden revelation. We are not threatened by the ground of being opening the skies and descending on us like a dove. It is we who are in quest, looking for God, looking here, looking there for God where we want to.

The Jesus of the Jesus movement is not the Christ who has been found, but the Christ who does the finding; he is the seeking and the saving Christ of the New Testament. But his appearance has been embarrassing because it is under the wrong auspices. Jesus has been breaking bread with sinners when he should have been breaking bread with us. Jesus has been mingling with drug addicts when he should have been attending the functions of churchmen. Jesus has been dealing with our children who left the Church — our children who have been finding him when we had successfully lost him. This is a curious, alarming, unnerving situation.

It is reported that there have been some colorful instances when "Jesus people" came into a church and stood beneath the pulpit and demanded that the preacher tell his experience of Jesus. This challenge symbolizes the predicament of the Church.

This Jesus who has been rediscovered is not an

expurgated Jesus. He is the Jesus whom we have rejected, the Jesus of the Gospel, of good news. He is Jesus the Christ, *Christos,* the anointed one, the deliverer, the savior. He is the one who has the power to do something in human life which we cannot do for ourselves, indeed, to do what has always been Gospel, to save God's people from their sins.

Therefore, if we are to speak of Jesus, the Christ, we now have to speak about sin. For a decade many Christians have been trying to reject the concept of sin. It can be eliminated by the plausible device of defining sin in such a way that it should be rejected, by defining sin as though it were essentially moral infraction, particularly moral rule infraction, infraction of the rules in the rule book.

Sin is not a moralistic category; it is a religious category. It is our state of contamination and lostness in the presence of the holy. There can be no understanding of sin without an awareness of the presence of God. When Christians lose their sense of sin, it is because they have lost their sense of God. Their sense of sin is in direct proportion to their sense of God. This becomes increasingly vivid when we realize that the revelation of God is incarnate in Jesus Christ. Sin is the contrast between the life of a man and the life of Christ. This is something those who first knew Jesus experienced. The disciples were aware of it. Peter says, "Depart from me for I am a sinful man, O Lord." The enemies of Christ wished to remove him because his presence, as well as his teaching, was a threat to their way of life. His teaching without its personification in his presence would have been no threat. The sentimental conception of Christ, or a purely moralistic one, as the ultimate good neighbor, does not convey this sense of "Christ's strange work" (Calvin), of his presence being judgment. The failure of the church to be clear about the reality of sin has made it irrelevant to the actual tragic experience of this moment.

If the Church has not been portraying sin, the secular artist has. One of the functions of art is to mirror the culture. If one goes to such a gallery as the Museum of Modern Art in New York, he is confronted by the vivid, perceiving presentation of the fraction, the anguish, the torment, the meaningless that the contemporary artist can portray with such power.

Recently I took a group of seminarians from Texas through the museum. One of them confessed an appalling sense of discomfort in the presence of this revelation. "I wanted to get out of there," he said. What is expressed in Picasso's *Guernica,* in Rouault's clowns, prostitutes and judges, in the crashing nightmare forms of Motherwell, is the agony of fallen human creation. If Christians are not talking about sin, the secular artist is making a statement about it without realizing what he is doing.

The drug addict may be the most vivid personification of the tragedy of our time. He has experienced in an acute form the anguish of the fall of modern man. Is it surprising that there, exactly there, has come an outbreak of awareness of sin and redemption? The addict can know full well that there has to be some answer to his predicament, to the human predicament, which is more than advice, therapy, human help and science. There has to be a savior. An experience of Christ has come at this point of desperation, suddenly and vividly.

It does not behoove church people in superiority to say this experience of salvation is not real. This has happened before; the reality of forgiveness through Christ can be felt and really known. The fact that church people have not been feeling it or knowing it for some time does not mean that it is unreal, but rather that the churchmen have been losing the gospel. The freedom of which the gospel speaks begins with the freedom of forgiveness. A Christian is not free because he has been able to persuade himself that he has no sin or that the very idea of sin is unreal, but because he knows that something has been done about his sin and that he can be restored and recreated in Christ.

Furthermore, this new advent of the forgiving Christ, the saving Lord, has reasserted an essential element of the gospel. The forgiveness of a person does not come from some edict of divinity, casually given because of his enormous good nature, but because God entered into human experience, took upon himself the anguish of our lot and gave himself utterly to the descent into the hell of our disaster. This saving deed produces the overpowering of the evil within ourselves, which we cannot control or conquer. The time has come for us to think again about the whole doctrine of redemption, particularly about the glorious theme of *Christus Victor*. This reconsideration is being forced upon us by the strange people who have been experiencing the living Christ.

But is there really "a Jesus movement?" We have heard of the "Jesus freaks," though most of us have never seen them. There have been great rallies, of a revivalistic nature, of hundreds of thousands of young people who have gathered under well-organized auspices. The graffiti in the subways of New York tell us that Jesus is "the only way."

Some of this interest may be media-made, but it is impossible to believe that it is all so. What seems obviously to have happened is that the current search for the transcendent has become indigenous. It is not natural for a young man from Peoria or Providence to become a Hindu, but there is a forgotten European and American transcendence, and it is in Jesus. Most of all, faith in Jesus works; it is an experienceable supernatural.

It is, however, not only the "true believer" who has recently become interested in Jesus. In the mid-60's Pasolini's *Gospel According to St. Matthew,* a literal film portrayal from the New Testament by an Italian Communist, arrested the attention of the entertainment world. The coming of *Godspell,* that winsome, loving picturing of Jesus, again using the literal Gospel words as text, pantomimed with the new techniques of story theater, has swept the United States and Europe. Both of these works demonstrate that twentieth century man can relate to this first century Christ.

A very different phenomenon is *Jesus Christ Superstar.*The lyrics are known by most American teenagers better than the Gospels. This bizarre and haunting rock opera is being accepted by millions as a portrayal of the real human Jesus. It asks the awful inescapable question about Jesus' identity: "Do you think you're what they say you are?" The merchants of entertainment are making millions on the project. Some of these productions of *Superstar* are blatantly blasphemous, a deliberate playing with the figure of Christ. But where there is blasphemy there is hope, for blasphemy cannot exist without some lurking sense of the holy to defame.

Superstar means that we cannot leave this Jesus alone. He is not the fading memory we feared he would become in the mid-60's. But before we can analyze the meaning of the present fascination that men feel for him in secular society, it may be gone. For a short time the Church has a new chance.

When the wind of the Spirit blows, it blows where it wills; it comes and it goes. And when God is active the demonic is always active too. The strange patterns of spiritual movement are understandable in Christian terms even if they are inscrutable to the secular observer. But when all of this is past, it will be found that one thing has been recovered, and that is the reality of religious experience. There has been a resurgence of a natural human and Christian necessity. We have begun to *feel* again in spiritual life. Now religious sensation has begun to come back, and not only to "Jesus freaks."

I had a wonderful conversation with a bishop who told me he had experienced an acute crisis of faith during the 60's until he was so shaken in his ministry that he feared he could not go on. He divulged this in great candor to his wife who said to him, "What do you do when somebody comes to you with this kind of problem?"

He said, "I tell him to pray through it."

And she said, "Then **you** pray through it."

He did, and suddenly he began to believe. That bishop has a strong and vital diocese. He is a man who understands religious experience, for he has experienced salvation by faith and of faith. This is the sort of moment that is likely to happen again and again in reaction to the difficulties we had in the theological revolution of the 60's. It is a cause for thanksgiving, but it is not enough. Faith restored through feeling must be followed by faith authenticated in mind.

In the eighteenth century there was the Wesleyan movement, which was "a Jesus movement." Anglicans handled it rather badly. Bishop Butler remarked to John Wesley that to pretend to special revelations of the Holy Spirit was "a horrid thing, a very horrid thing." The Methodists split off then. It is important that this not happen again. Having said this, let me say another thing. In the controversy, the Anglicans were right in mind, even if wrong in heart.

"Enthusiasm," as it was then called, the assurance in faith by immediate experience, is not enough. Instant experience, whether of conversion, sanctification, mystical moments, whatever they may be, is transitory. It is likely to be followed by all kinds of dark nights of the soul — also God's gift, but nonetheless destructive unless they are experienced within the community of Christians, unless they are experienced with some undergirding of mind as well as feeling, unless they are experienced in sacramental communion that actually deals with bread, wine, body, blood, with the corporeality of the human nature as well as its spirituality. We must be sacramentally sustained in body as well as in soul so that we may persist, persist as individuals, persist as Church, persist even as small groups of specially blessed people from one year to another and from one generation to another, and from one gift of the Holy Spirit to another. Therefore, it is necessary for the churches like ours to become alive to the responsibility of being attractive, open, and available to the new Christians, to incorporate them into the ongoing sacramental power of the Christian community. And all of this must be thought through, theologized.

The intellectual experience of Christ is just as authentic as the emotional experience of Christ. There have been two great tendencies in recent theological thought, which focus on the ultimate dimensions of Jesus and which could contribute much to the understanding of the new Christians, expanding their perception of the meaning of

Christ from a purely private experience into an awareness of his total meaning. In a sense they are also Jesus movements.

There is the Jesus movement started by Teilhard de Chardin. The thought of this paleontologist-priest has helped thousands to recover the awareness of the cosmic Christ in terms of evolution. Christians of all confessions have been led by him to a repossession of the New Testament faith that Jesus has a meaning not only for individuals, and for religion, but for all that there is: that he is in a very concrete sense the alpha and omega of creation. The prodigious creativity of this self-sacrificing, brave, and brilliant Jesuit in the face of persecution in his own church brought again to Western Christians a sense of Jesus which the Eastern Orthodox Church had never lost. The present interest in Jesus needs to be fulfilled in this kind of dimension, so that Jesus is not just a personal savior, but the Lord whom we expect to effect the transfiguration of the cosmos in resurrection glory.

The theology of hope is another Jesus movement, though its German authors might be startled to hear it called this. It is a reaffirmation of the actuality of the resurrection and its consequences in secular society and eschatology. Pannenberg, Moltmann, and Metz, young theologians of genius, can give the new disciples of Jesus, who are sometimes deficient in social conscience, an insight into the revolutionary consequences of believing in a dying and rising savior.

Pannenberg has produced a stunning fresh

apologetic for the resurrection in his *Jesus — God and Man,* probably the finest work in theology in a decade. The theologians of hope point to the resurrection of Jesus as an absolutely unique event, the advent of the totally new, which is the foretaste of the inevitable future of mankind when Christ must reign till he has put all enemies under his feet. In the meantime, the meantime which is now, we must actualize this reign of Christ in the world. The gospel of the resurrection means that the newness which happens in Christ is the pattern of the future. It is God's own thrust into history which is to bring in an absolutely new era of freedom and justice, so Christians must identify with every movement which moves toward that goal, put their bodies where the action must be for the changing of social order in expectation of the coming future which is Christ's. The theology of hope is not just a yearning: it issues in the Christian hope being acted out now.

The most powerful force within the Church at this moment is the "charismatic movement." It is a great surge of awareness of the Holy Spirit, sometimes pentecostal in its form, always an intense revival of vital prayer and the awareness of God's working. What has been happening has again taken the Church by surprise. It has emerged as a "gut reaction" against the denial of the supernatural, as an almost visceral protest against the thwarting of the experience of the transcendent.

Suddenly, without our wanting it, there has sprung up a strange stirring — men have been speaking in tongues. Is it a new Pentecost, or a psychological derangement? What are we to make of it? Well, presumably what was made of it in the New Testament. When the Holy Spirit comes upon a man or upon a church, he is out of control — or rather under the control of God. Something wells up that may very well have a physical expression.

Glossolalia is a gift, a gift that comes, a gift that goes. The Church is still the Church when there is no glossolalia. A man can be baptized with the Spirit if there is no glossolalia; if he is baptized with water, he is baptized with the Spirit. There is only one baptism. At this moment, particularly after the recent arid history of spiritual experience in the Church, the Spirit in fulfilment of baptism may express itself in strange new forms that may seem embarrassing.

We have to return to the apostle Paul to learn again what speaking in tongues means. He did it himself; in fact, he declared that he spoke in tongues more than anyone else in the Church. It appears as a kind of praying in the Spirit. But while he valued the gift, he realized that it had to be tested. It could be a sign of the working of the Spirit, or it could be a source of divisiveness, a claim of superiority, a danger ever present when this gift appears. Read again Paul's First Letter to the Corinthians. We often forget that the 13th chapter is about tongues. "Though I speak with tongues of men and of angels" is about tongues. Whether glossolalia is of the Spirit or "sounding brass or a tinkling cymbal" depends on whether it results in love. It is the fruits of the Spirit that identify the presence of the Spirit, and the fruits of the Spirit come to one thing only — Christ is formed in us. This is the permanent test for discerning the Spirit.

The charismatic movement has focused the attention of the Church on the Holy Spirit, but it has had a tendency to concentrate too exclusively on the experiential aspects of the Holy Spirit. There is more to the Spirit than being moved, either as individuals or in groups. There are infinite dimensions to the life of the Spirit. In the history of the Church the theology of the Spirit has been neglected, though more in the Western than in the Eastern church. Now, as seldom before, we need thought as well as feeling concerning this doctrine. We need an intellectual experience of the Spirit as much as an intellectual experience of Christ. In this enterprise we must return to the sources, to the New Testament, the Fathers and the Eastern Christian tradition, and from all this begin again. We need the Holy Spirit to enlighten us about the doctrine of the Holy Spirit — this will be truly a "new theology"!

The religious history of the past decade has gone from the secularization of Christianity to Pentecostalism.

God has been disturbing his Church again. He has made us think anxiously about him, even about his very existence. In the anguish of questioning and even unbelief, he has made us realize that he is necessary to our life. Now, for a season, has come an outpouring of new assurance to many Christians who have found a repossession of faith. Once again Jesus Christ and the Holy Spirit are vivid in the consciousness of Christians.

It is possible to sense that in all of this we are in the grip of a divine action to which we must respond, alive and alert to its meaning. Christ is being made known to us by the Spirit; the Charismatic Christ is being revealed in the mind and heart of the Church. This is theology in its deepest sense; this is the knowledge of God.

COME HOLY SPIRIT!

A. M. Allchin

5. *Christ and the Spirit*

The theme of our conference has been "The Charismatic Christ," and my particular topic is "The Charismatic Christ, the Christian and the Cosmos"; in other words Christ the giver of the Spirit, the Christian the one who lives in Christ, and the whole created order. It is an utterly relevant theme. We are living at a moment when the figure of Jesus Christ has come alive for a great many people in a great many unexpected ways. It is also a time in which many believe that we can see a new outpouring of the gifts of the Spirit. But it is also a time when the ruthless and unthinking ways in which we have exploited this planet, the bit of the universe we know best and that has been entrusted to our care, has suddenly made us pause. Ecology, the environment, these have suddenly become everybody's words. How should man relate to the world around him? Can we learn a new respect for the material substance of this planet? Will the human race be able to survive at all unless we learn this new respect? Or is it perhaps a question of recovering an earlier respect and reverence for things, so that we can begin again to see the world as holy, a sacrament of unsuspected realities?

It is not only the question of the environment that has brought this longing to see creation as holy to the fore. In a time like ours, when many feel that God has hidden himself — and I suppose that we all feel that at times — the longing after God can take many forms. In particular it can express itself as a longing to see at least some glimpse of his glory in creation. I want to quote from the work of one of the most perceptive commentators on the deeper movements of our time, Professor Nathan A. Scott, professor both in the Divinity School and in the School of English in the University of Chicago, and Canon of St. James' Cathedral in that city. In his recent book, *The Wild Prayer of Longing,* he writes:

> One feels, wherever one turns in this strange, late time, that, beneath the flamboyance and antinomianism which are everywhere rampant, the prompting passion by which men are today coming more and more to be most deeply moved is a great need - in the absence of God - to find the world in which we dwell to be, nevertheless, in some sort truly a sacramental economy, where to be "with it" is to be "with" a sacred reality. We are, it would seem, a people whose most imperious desire is to win the assurance that Moses was given near Mt. Sinai, that the place whereon we stand is holy ground. [9]

At the end of the same book, Nathan Scott sums up the whole course of his argument by speaking of what, in his understanding,

> is of the very essence of the sacramental principle
> — namely, that nothing may be a sacrament, unless
> everything is, at bottom, sacramental, and that ours
> may be considered to be a sacramental universe,
> because in its every aspect and dimension it is
> (despite all the appearances, one might add) in-
> stinct with that which. . .is for man rather than
> against him.[10]

It hardly needs to be said how closely this vision of the whole universe as sacramental corresponds to what Fr. Alexander Schmemann has said in his book *The World as Sacrament,* and to Fr. Michael Marshall's insistence that we need to loosen up our "tight sacramentalism" by seeing it in its whole context. We live in a sacramental universe, instinct in every part with what is for man rather than against him; a universe full of the activities of God, where all things work together for good to those who love God. It is a world in every part capable of being known as God's gift and God's word to us, at least capable of being known in that way when we receive it in and through Jesus Christ who is the supreme gift, the supreme Word of God to us and to all men.

Is this a new way of perceiving the reality of Christ? It may be for us, for very often we have forgotten the cosmic dimensions of the person of our redeemer. It would not have seemed strange to St. Paul. The Father, he tells us, rescued us from darkness and brought us "into the Kingdom of his dear Son, in whom our release is secured and our sins forgiven. He is the image of the invisible God; his is the primacy over all created things. In him everything in heaven and on earth was created...the whole universe has been created through him and for him." (Colossians 1:13-16) It would not have seemed strange to the author of the Epistle to the Hebrews. "...In this final age God has spoken to us in the Son whom he made heir to the whole universe and through whom he created all orders of existence: the Son who is the effulgence of God's splendor and the stamp of God's very being, and sustains the universe by his word of power." (Hebrews 1:2-3) It would certainly not have seemed strange to St. John. "The Word then, was with God in the beginning, and through him all things came to be.... All that came to be was alive with his life, and that light was the life of men. The light shines on in the dark, and the darkness has never mastered it." (John 1:2-5) Here at the very heart of the New Testament is the affirmation that in some way, however mysterious, Jesus Christ, the one who had lived and taught and healed and suffered and died and risen from the dead, the one whom they had known, was him in whom the whole universe holds together. In him, God's secret purpose for all things is revealed.

If one were speaking directly out of the tradition of the Eastern Orthodox Church, it would be easy to bring a crowd of witnesses to speak of this theme of the cosmic Christ. For in Eastern Christianity, this vision has always remained central and

alive, as it was in the greatest of the Greek fathers.
But if we turn to the most influential of nineteenth
century Anglican theologians, F. D. Maurice, we
shall find the same thing. Being nearer to our own
time than the biblical writers, he speaks more in
terms of process and development and thinks
more about man's work of scientific discovery, but
the affirmation is the same.

> All living processes, be they slow or rapid, be they
> carried on in the womb of nature, or through the
> intervention of human art — have their first power
> and principle in him; without him, nothing could
> become that does become. Such a belief carries us
> into great depths and heights. It increases the
> wonder with which we regard every dynamic
> discovery. . . . It gives direction and depth to the
> investigations of science. . . . The Word, who is the
> light of men, will himself teach those who seek
> humbly and diligently to enter into those oper-
> ations of life of which he is the first mover.[11]

This Lord Christ who is present in all things,
whose activities are to be discerned in all events
and in all situations, is not some other one than
the one historic person of Jesus of Nazareth of
whom the Gospels speak. Rather it is he who by
his smallest action reveals to us the true law, the
true nature of our being. Commenting on the
miracles in St. John's Gospel, F.D. Maurice says
that these signs "testify that there is an invisible
power at work in all the springs of our life — that
there is a fountain of life from which those springs
are continually refreshed and renewed," and
speaking of the healing of the blind man through

clay and spittle, a very material operation, he adds,
"does not this sign testify that there is a potency
and virtue in the very commonest things; that God
has stored all nature with instruments for the
blessing and healing of his creatures?"[12] The contrast between this vision of things and our own
common view of a universe polluted and de-
spoiled by the greed and exploitation of man is so
sharp as to be almost unbearable. We often feel in
our own time that the very elements of the world
are turning against us; they no longer work with
us but rather take revenge upon us for our
thoughtless exploitation of them. Shall we be able
to rediscover a true attitude towards material
things, unless we can find them redeemed and
healed in Christ, marked by the sign of his death
and resurrection?

How can it be, that in one man there is this key
to unlock the secrets of the universe? The scandal
of particularity, the once-for-all uniqueness of
God's deed in Jesus Christ, is perhaps the deepest
mystery of our faith. We shall not even begin to
enter into it unless we begin to understand something about the catholicity, the universality of the
human person. Each one of us when we begin to
live a truly human, a truly personal life as opposed
to a self-sufficient, individual existence, can open
out into a dimension of universality. The image
and likeness of God in which we are made begins
to be realized in us. The individual seeks to hug
the common nature to himself, he lives by opposi-
tion, by being over against, by self-justification
and self-assertion. The person knows that the

nature is common to all. He lives by communion, not by separation. He loses his life in order to find it. He finds in every man, a man after his own heart, a brother; he finds the whole universe full of friendly powers. We think, just for an example, of St. Francis in his relationship to all men, all living creatures, all things.

A man who is filled with this Christlike love, with the love of God himself, finds that like God he is *for* all men, not against them. He can love even his enemies. He can forgive even himself. Metropolitan Anthony in his most recent book, *Meditations on a Theme,* speaks about this in a very practical way.

I remember how impressed I was at the moment of the invasion of Czechoslovakia, when I met Dr. Hromadka, one of the leaders of the Church in that country. I had known him for many years, and when we met he said to me; 'Tell everyone not to hate our invaders for love of us; those who hate the ones for the sake of the others give a free hand to the devil.' He was engaged, and committed to the fight, yet he knew where the real battle took place, in the hearts of men, between love and hatred, light and darkness, God and him who is the murderer from the beginning. To choose some in order to love them, to reject others in order to hate them, whichever side you take, only adds to the sum total of hatred and darkness. And the devil finds his own profit in it; he does not mind whom you hate; once you hate, you have opened a door for him to walk through, to creep into your heart, to invade a human situation. The love which Christ teaches us is incompatible with hatred of the other, we must learn to "discern the Spirit of God from the spirit of the prince of this world," and the touchstone is humility and selfless love. And love includes myself also.[13]

That is the word indeed to our polarised world.

The man in whom this love of Christ is at work, the love of him who told us to love our enemies, finds that in a mysterious way the human person is catholic, universal; one man is every man, all men are one man. When I pray, all men pray in me. When I enter into communion with God, I find the whole universe he has created, all mankind whom he loves. You can find very much about this in the later and still largely unexplored writings of Thomas Merton: in *Conjectures of a Guilty Bystander,* in *The Climate of Monastic Prayer,* in *Contemplation in a World of Action.* For these are insights given as a man is prepared in stillness and in silence to let the vision of things, and of God, grow and deepen in him; as he is prepared to regard the world with eyes of wonder, respect and love, not simply with the eyes of possessive and manipulative desire. There are very many today, not only among the young, but predominantly among them, who are beginning to perceive the profound imbalance that prevails in our technological society. They are seeking to recover the way of silence, contemplation, the growth in inner life, the hidden celebration of the heart, over against the noisy, often futile activism with which the world is filled. We must go inward, recover the great tradition of prayer and spirituallty which is there within the Christian tradition. We must seek to understand how it relates to the experience of prayer in the other religious traditions of mankind. There, if we seek it, in the inner life, hidden with Christ in God, shall we find the full dimensions of the human heart. The human heart can go to the lengths of God; the human heart and mind are of such great, such infinite capacity if only we will give ourselves to God, to find our heart in his heart.

Here again we must be careful not to dissociate things that belong together. The hidden Christ of the heart, the light within which we find when in silence we enter into the deep of our being, is not another Christ from the incarnate Christ of the Gospels, the Christ who comes to us in the sacraments of the Church, the Christ we meet in our neighbor, and especially in the one who is poor, neglected, illtreated, misused. At all costs let us avoid replacing one slogan by another, taking up with a new gimmick instead of an old one. Yesterday it was urban crisis; today it is charismatic renewal. Yesterday it was Christ in the inner city, today it is Christ in our inner experience. Holy worldliness is out; psychedelic celebration is in. What nonsense this would be. The fearful problems of our world and our society, racial harmony, economic justice, international understanding, the humanization of vast and impersonal systems have not gone away because for a moment we have turned our attention to other things. What we have to learn, maybe, is that we need to be able to stand back from them, so as to find the vision and the power that will enable us to tackle them afresh.

But there is one Christ, one Lord, and he comes to us in many ways and many guises. We shall need to find him in many ways. We need a renewal of the Church's tradition of prayer and silence, and discipline of life, to respond to the longing of our day for a true and living spirituality. We need no less a renewal of the prayer of congregations and communities, liturgical, sacramental prayer. The two are not opposed but complementary. We need a renewed love and study of the Bible, not as an archaic text, but as that which will speak to us of the living Christ, directly in the New Testament, by way of longing and expectation in the Old. It is through the reading of the scripture that we shall find the basis of both corporate and personal prayer and meditation. We need a renewal of the Church's ministry of service in all the places of our world where darkness reigns, where men find themselves cast out, oppressed, deprived of human worth, where men suffer every kind of hunger from physical to spiritual. Christ comes to us in many ways.He has promised to be with us thus, and we shall not find him in the one unless we find him in the other. We cannot find him who suffered and died in the nakedness of a public execution if we seek to hide ourselves away from the griefs and sufferings, the fearful blindnesses of our age. But we cannot go into the world to do deeds of love and deeds of justice in his name, unless we are learning to find within, in prayer and silence, in meditation and reflection, the power that comes from God, the power of humble love, the love that is able to love our enemies. Nor shall we find him within or in the world, unless we are constantly and faithfully turning to him, the historic Christ, where he comes to us in his word, in his sacraments, so that our life is being united with his life, built up into the pattern of his death and rising, his triumph over death by death.

We need all these things. But can we find them, or make them for ourselves? No, not for an instant in our own power, our own cleverness; only in Christ, the one who comes to us from the Father, the charismatic Christ, the one who gives gifts to men, above all the one who gives the gift of the Spirit, God himself given to us; God himself in us, with us, between us, among us, around us, beside us and always beyond us, always leading us on. *O heavenly king, O Comforter, the Spirit of truth, you are in all places, you fill all things, come and abide in us, cleanse us from all filth, of your goodness establish and make firm our lives in you.*

For if Christ is in all things, so too is the Spirit. The Father uses in our creation his two hands of love, the Son and the Spirit. And just as the one Christ, the Jesus of Bethlehem and Nazareth, of the cross tree and the lakeside dawn, is the Word in whom all things cohere, so the one Spirit, the Lord who gives life to all things and is present in all places, is also the unique and unrepeatable gift, given to each one, at the inmost hidden place of the heart, the white stone with a name in it which no man knows save him to whom it is given, at the very heart and ground of our being. So the one Spirit who gathers us together into one also gives different gifts to each human person, crowning each one with the unspeakable joy of his presence.

Let us thank God that we are living at a time when very many are being led to ask anew for the gifts of the Spirit, are finding new manifestations of his power. Let us pray that we who have received that Spirit in baptism and confirmation, and in the gift of ordination, may not be faithless to what we have received, but may live by the gift which is ours, may so stir up the Spirit which is within us that we may be at the service of those around us who have been moved by the Spirit, to help them to grow in the gift they have received, to discern between what is from the Spirit of God and what from the spirits of illusion, to discern between what is from the Spirit of God and what is from the spirit of man. Here again there is in Christianity a great treasure of wisdom and experience, available to us if only we will turn to it, which we need to make our own, so that it may grow, adapt itself and change to meet the needs of our own time, relate itself to the researches and discoveries of our contemporaries into the inner world of man.

For we know how easy it is to become dead to the prompting of God's Spirit, to lack sensitivity and vision for the work of the Spirit in us and around us. We know that, for the most part, we have everything to learn in truly understanding and aiding the growth of the gifts the Spirit gives. You will remember that in the passage from Archbishop Anthony, which I quoted earlier, he ended with the words, "The love which Christ teaches us is incompatible with hatred of the other, we must learn to 'discern the Spirit of God from the spirit of the prince of this world,' and the touchstone is humility and selfless love." Humility and selfless love; do we find these qualities in ourselves or in others, when we or they claim to have the gift of the Spirit of Christ? Are we being led by the Spirit to true humility? Do we even know what it is? To love all men, including our nearest and our farthest enemies, do we even know what that is?

These two signs of which the Archbishop speaks are to be found wonderfully described in the writings of Staretz Silvan, one from whom the Archbishop has, I know, learned much. How good it is that an Archbishop, a cultivated man, a doctor of medicine, a man of much travel, should be glad to be the disciple of a lay monk, a peasant who never went beyond the second grade in a village school in prerevolutionary Russia, and who lived all his adult life in and around the Russian monastery on Mount Athos. But then in the Church, as in true humanity, professional titles and qualifications are not of all that much account. The apostles did not have very many. From the old man (for "staretz" is simply the Russian word for "old man") there is much that we too can learn.

There is a wide difference between the simplest man who has come to know the Lord by the Holy

Spirit, and even a great man ignorant of the grace of the Holy Spirit. There is a big distinction between merely believing that God exists, in seeing him in nature or in the Scriptures, and knowing the Lord by the Holy Spirit. The spirit of the man who has come to know God by the Holy Spirit burns day and night with love to God, and his soul can find no earthly attachment.[14]

We ought not to be surprised if the first vivid awakening of the life of the Spirit within sometimes throws people into confusion or some kind of ecstasy. When the finger of God touches us, all the hidden springs of our being may be unloosed. But it is important as we go on, to learn to distinguish the surface manifestations, the excitement and exultation, the utterance and enthusiasm, from the deeper abiding realities, the peace and hope, the quiet joy in the Spirit. Above all we shall look, in ourselves and in others, for some real growth in the life of prayer and in the spirit of humble, active love.

The man who has the Holy Spirit within him, in however slight a degree, prays day and night for all mankind, and sorrows in their sorrow.His heart is filled with pity for all God's creatures, and more especially for those who do not know God or who resist him. . . . For them, more than for himself, he prays night and day, that all may repent and know the Lord." [15]

And in a more daring expression, "God is love, and the Holy Spirit in the saints is love. Dwelling in the Holy Spirit, the saints behold hell and embrace it too, in their love."[16]

This unspeakable gift, God himself in us and with us, is the source of an unquenchable joy and a new and paradoxical freedom of life. Where the Spirit of the Lord is, there is liberty. And yet this most personal, inward reality is also the power that joins us all together into one. The gift of tongues at Pentecost was given for the healing and reconciliation of the nations, scattered abroad under the curse of Babel. The Spirit who is the Spirit of joy and exultation, of praise and thanksgiving, is also the Spirit of wisdom and understanding, of awe and sobriety, of gentleness and attention to others. The Spirit works in many ways, and we should be wise not to judge too quickly whether he is present or absent by any one, immediately applicable criterion. Hear the Staretz again and note his balance.

> In heaven all things live and move by the Holy Spirit. But this same Holy Spirit is on earth too. The Holy Spirit lives in the Church; in the Sacraments; in the Holy Scriptures; in the hearts of believers. The Holy Spirit unites all men; (here and beyond the bounds of death) and so the saints are close to us; and when we pray with them they hear our prayer in the Holy Spirit and we feel that they are praying for us."[17]

I find it difficult to believe that the prayers of the old man who wrote that, and who died in 1938, are not still with us now. For in the power of the Spirit who unites us in love the boundaries of death are overpassed, and our prayer is carried up with his, through Jesus Christ our Lord, to the Father. And I want, if I may, to end by handing on to you the form of prayer around which the Staretz Silvan will have formed his own life. It is a form of prayer very familiar to Eastern Orthodox Christians and increasingly familiar to Christians of every tradition. It is a narrow door, which opens out into a large place, a form of prayer adapted to people at all stages of life's way, which can be used at all times, in all circumstances. As we use it, it only gradually reveals its many dimensions. I speak of the Jesus Prayer. It is a prayer that centers upon our personal encounter with the Lord Christ, that brings God and man together in a relationship of mercy and love, that will help us to see the Lord as present in all things, speaking to us in every moment. In its essence it is very simple. It consists of the constant, quiet repetition of the words:

Lord Jesus Christ, Son of God, have mercy on me a sinner.

I believe that this prayer, if it were to enter into the hearts and minds of all of us, and of Christians of every kind, would do more for true unity than any other one thing. It would bring together young and old, radical and conservative, charismatic and pentecostal, into the single point where we all meet, the Christ who is the giver of the Spirit, the Christ who teaches us to say, Abba, Father.

Every time that we come to pray it is a new beginning, a starting out on something new, fresh, without precedent. For always the mystery of God reveals itself to us in some new dimension, calls us into a newness of life. We do not know what to pray for as we ought; before the mystery and majesty of God we are always infants, without a word; but the Spirit himself pleads for us with groanings that go beyond words. Perhaps the prayer we may make for ourselves at the end of this Conference is this

O Lord, even if I have done nothing good in your sight, and in your sight all that I have done is less than nothing, yet grant me according to your grace, to make a beginning of good. May it be so. Amen.

A Sermon for Priests

6. *Receive the Holy Spirit*

ROBERT E. TERWILLIGER

Late that Sunday evening, when the disciples were together behind closed doors, for fear of the Jews, Jesus came and stood among them. 'Peace be with you!' he said, and then showed them his hands and his side. So when the disciples saw the Lord, they were filled with joy. Jesus repeated, 'Peace be with you!', and said, 'As the Father sent me, so I send you.' Then he breathed on them, saying, 'Receive the Holy Spirit! If you forgive any man's sins, they stand forgiven; if you pronounce them unforgiven, unforgiven they remain.'.

John 20: 19-23

The risen Christ commissions his apostles with the words, "Receive the Holy Spirit." These words of the Jesus of the Fourth Gospel pertain to the apostolic ministry. As they were said to the apostles, so were they said to us. Such words as these were spoken at our ordination.

Remember, visualize, that moment when the bishop laid his hands upon our heads. Remember, visualize, that moment when we were made priests of God by the power of the Spirit. By this gift of the Spirit, we have been made givers of the Spirit. Let us now penitently, and in holy fear, realize what this means. But first — we are doing this as an act of Eucharist; let us sense what the Eucharist can show us about the gift of the Spirit.

At the center of the eucharistic action, in the midst of the Prayer of Consecration, there is the invocation of the Holy Spirit, the *epiclesis.*

But what does the *epiclesis* mean? Is it some sort of trinitarian politeness in prayer? Is it simply liturgical pattern making? "Come Holy Spirit" — it seems so easy to invoke the Holy Spirit.

Perhaps we can break through to the awful meaning of *epiclesis* if we ask this strange question: What did the Holy Spirit cost? What did the Holy Spirit cost Christ? The gift which he gave with these words, "Receive the Holy Spirit" — what did it cost Christ? It cost his prayer.

The Fourth Gospel is the great New Testament book of the Spirit. It is the life of Christ written in the light of the experience of the Holy Spirit in the earliest church. It is even more a book of the Spirit than the Acts of the Apostles because it is written later and is informed by a longer and deeper experience of the Spirit. The Fourth Gospel is also the book of the prayer of Christ. There in the words of the praying Christ we come to know the meaning of his very being as he spreads forth his life before God and before us. The Christ of the

Fourth Gospel at the Last Supper promises, after his passion and glorification, to pray the Father to send the Spirit upon the church.

What is this prayer of Christ? Prayer is quite obviously not something that we say at God, our advice to God. Jesus is not just promising to suggest to God that he should do something wonderful for the apostles. It is something stupendously different. Jesus will ask God to give them his very being. What right will he have to do that? It is the right that comes from the only prayer there is — the real life and the real will that are offered to God.

The prayer of Christ is the life of Christ. In the pattern of the Fourth Gospel the prayer for the Spirit is the result of the passion of Christ. Jesus promises this intercession as he is ready to go into the act of death, into the act of utter self-giving, to the shedding of blood, to the cry of dereliction, to the ghastliness, the lostness, the descent into hell. What did the Holy Spirit cost? The Christ who prays the Father for the gift of the Spirit is the Christ who has fulfilled his obedience to the Father's will. The gift of the Spirit cost the cross of Christ, his going down into nothingness for us. This is his prayer for the gift of the Spirit. And God accepts it by raising him from the dead.

This is all reflected in the Prayer of Consecration. The *anamnesis* precedes the *epiclesis.* The recalling of Christ preceds the invocation of the Holy Spirit. The *anamnesis,* the recalling, should not be thought of simply as an easy recollection of Jesus, but as our bringing of Christ

before the Father through our prayer, our plead-
ing of all that he did and all that he is, as he
presents himself to the Father having fulfilled his
self-offering. What we are recalling into the presence of God is not just Christ's teaching, not just
the memory of a beautiful person, but his suffering, his death, his mighty resurrection, his glorious
ascension. We are re-calling into the presence of
God that Christ who has a right to ask God to pour
out the Holy Spirit upon the church. In the
deepest sense the *anamnesis* and the *epiclesis* are
one; the *anamnesis* is the *epiclesis*. It cost Christ
his life to pray for the Spirit. Every giving of the
Spirit is at the cost of the cross. This is the cost of
the invocation of the Holy Spirit. By the gift of the
Holy Spirit come the body and blood of Christ; by
the body and blood of Christ comes the gift of the
Holy Spirit. This is the perpetual pattern of the
Eucharist; this is the perpetual pattern of the
church. "Receive the Holy Spirit" — the risen
Christ shows the disciples his wounded hands and
his side as he breathes upon them the Spirit.

Then what happened? In these days when we
have an awakened sense of the Holy Spirit, perhaps we should realize that the most important
thing about the stories of the gift of the Spirit is in
the human transformation it caused. The wonder
of the tales of the Acts of the Apostles is not to be
found in amazing and terrifying events of mighty
wind and fire, with some peculiar kind of utterance; it is revealed in the incredible thing that
happened to those impossible people.

The power of the Spirit is manifest in the conquest of the weirdness of the apostles. We know all too much about them, which is one of the reasons for us to have hope. We know about Peter, the chief of them. We know that he was an impulsive man, volatile and unstable.

We know the Apostolic Church. We know that even when the apostles sat there in the presence of the living Lord, they simply sat there, stunned, startled — sat. Then something happened to them, something that produced an absolute revolution in their psyches and their beings that turned these inadequate, uneducated men into the persuaders and the convincers of the world. And we know another thing, too — this keeps happening. In every generation it keeps happening.

Look at this place in which we are meeting, Riverside Church, and think of it in terms of the Holy Spirit. This building was built for one man, a preacher. It housed his congregation. He was a man who had a peculiar responsibility, and though he may not have been what we would call an orthodox Christian, he had a tremendous vocation to make men able to know Christ and at the same time maintain intellectual integrity, and that is a work of the Spirit.

But Riverside Church does not look like Harry Emerson Fosdick; it looks very much like Chartres Cathedral — and that is no accident. You sit under the exact reproductions of the windows of the most beautiful church in Christendom. The people who built this church wanted something that reminded them of the way the Spirit moved in the thirteenth century. They lived in an amazingly successful technological society. They also felt the urgent need to escape from the meaning-lessness of technology. So, they took a neo-Gothic trip. They found that there was something in Gothic glory that gave them reassurance. They wanted to feel the Spirit as he moved in the Middle Ages. They yearned for the sense of transcendent meaning he created in the mystery of medieval worship.

As a teenager I came in here. I could not go to Europe. Yet here Europe came to me with all its holy history, and I felt the Christian continuity surge within my blood. This is one of the churches that made me an Anglican. This is the kind of thing that happens. The miracle that happens again and again. You have yours, and I have mine. In every generation this strange thing happens.

Dean Church once wrote an amazing essay on how, when the gospel hit various cultures, every one of them became alive with a new life, with a vitality that was astounding. This is the miracle of the Spirit taking the strange, human things that God has made and that have fallen and recreating them, refashioning them, cleansing them, bring-ing them into transfiguration. This is the miracle of the Spirit. And the bishop laid hands on our heads and said, "Receive it."

How did we think of ordination when it hap-pened? Did we realize what would later happen to us? Many of us are going through an identity crisis about priesthood. The source of that crisis is varied. One cure for that crisis is to recover what ordination really is. It is not simply the confirming of a professional status, but a supernatural sacramental gift, the making of a sacramental person.

What is a sacrament? Surely baptism. What is baptism? Baptism is washing in the name of the Holy Trinity. You have done it, time and time again you have done it. You have told people, and they have believed you, that the child whom you baptized received the Holy Spirit. From these hands children have received the Holy Spirit, adults have received the Holy Spirit. That is what we have said, and that is what we have believed. Part of the problem is, that when we have baptized someone we may have thought something like this: We have "done" another baptism. Or perhaps even worse, the child is "done." This mistake comes partially from our rather absurd Western Christian way of thinking of sacramental validity — what is the least possible thing to be done in order for the Holy Spirit to get through.

A sacrament is something begun, not something completed. It is something begun. Ordination was begun in us when the bishop laid hands upon our heads. That was to empower us to do what? The day before your ordination you may have wondered about this.

I remember walking with a friend, who was in seminary with me, the day before his ordination. He had a seizure of common sense and did not want to be ordained. He knew that before him there was a vast unknown. There was something that he could not do. He was right. When we were given the Holy Spirit in ordination it was because we could not do it. If you feel inadequate to your ministry that is simply the truth. It is not we who are supposed to effect the ministry of Christ. It is Christ by the power of the Spirit that effects his ministry through us.

The Spirit is given in ordination for the ministry of the sacraments. Right now in the Church we have liturgical revival. We must not lose the liturgy as we have the revival. We must realize the effect of the liturgy does not depend upon the arrangements we make or the modernity of our form, though arrangements should be sensible and forms should be contemporary. The effectiveness depends upon the actualization of Christ.

The most important thing in our celebration of the Eucharist is not how beautifully or how ingeniously we do it, but *that we should know what we are doing!* If we realize with awe that we are actually the agents of the Lord God, no matter in what form we celebrate, we shall not be an obstacle to his grace, to his Spirit. This realization will communicate itself instantly to the congregation.

Even as we are the vehicles of the Spirit, so can we be obstructions to the Spirit. If there is one thing that I would plead with you, it would be simply this: Do not go into your sacramental actions unaware, unaware of the awfulness of what you are doing, unaware of the awfulness that we have been commissioned to perform. There must be something within you of that tremendous sense of need — not of adequacy, but of need — which will communicate itself to your people. And the joy of the liturgy is the satisfaction of that need in the transcendent mystery of the sacraments.

The Spirit is also given in ordination for the ministry of the Word. We are commissioned to preach. We are commissioned to proclaim the gospel of God. Preaching is almost dead in our church. We have even come to the point of thinking that there should be some substitute for the ministry of the Word, something more ingenious, something more relevant. No!

The one strange new thing from the pulpit that would electrify people of God would be the Gospel. It is the Gospel we have been commissioned and empowered to preach. But we do not preach effectively quite simply because we have not received the word of God before we attempt to proclaim it. Preaching requires stillness, openness, and, above all, penitence. Preaching requires an awareness that what we offer is something by which we ourselves are being transformed.

True Christian preaching is an instrument for social transformation. It has been one of the greatest powers for change the world has ever known. But remember this: It cannot effectively motivate people to engage in great and dangerous causes unless the preacher has within him a sense of a Word from the Lord to which he must witness — conceivably alone and at the cost of his own life. This comes only from the awareness that his life does not belong to him, that he has been bought with a price and his obedience is his thanksgiving. When this is within his very being, he can speak and he can convince.

The Church is now in great danger. It is in great danger because it is so boring. It is in great danger because it is so dreary. It is in great danger because it is so dull. The Church has been made boring and dreary and dull by us who are supposed to have received the Holy Spirit but who manifest no fire.

You have come to this place from all over this nation. Many of you have come at great cost to yourselves. I have spoken these words to you not in condemnation, but in hope because you have come. You have come in numbers that we could never have predicted. You have come, and you have received again something of the gift of the Spirit.

Now you are going back into your parishes, to those places from which you may have fled for a moment. You have to go back. When you return, remember that you are where God put you, and that your ordination was a commission and a beginning, and keep receiving the Holy Spirit with power. You are not going there alone. You have no idea what power is in you. When you see that God is calling you to do something, to say something, to be something in that place, then rely on the Holy Spirit — for you have been ordained.

The gift has been given. Let it happen to you.

You need no other gift than what has been put within you, nothing less than the very God himself. Therefore, in the name of Christ who bought this gift with his own life, be faithful to him and set men free. "If you forgive any man's sins, they stand forgiven;" "This is my body," "this is my blood" — set men free. *In the name of the Father, and of the Son, and of the Holy Spirit.* Amen.

NOTES

[1] Harvey Cox, *The Feast of Fools* (Cambridge, Massachusetts: Harvard University Press, 1969), p. 120.

[2] *The Church for Others* (Geneva: World Council of Churches, 1967), p. 18.

[3] Hans Urs von Balthasar, *A Theology of History* (New York: Sheed & Ward, Inc., 1963), pp. 132ff.

[4] See Nicholas Zernov, *The Church of the Eastern Christians* (New York: Macmillan Company, 1942), p. 54. "The East does not think about salvation in terms of the individual soul returning to its maker; it is visualized rather as a gradual process of transfiguration of the whole cosmos. . . Man is saved not from the world, but into the world, because he is its guardian and master."

[5] Harvey Cox, *The Secular City* (New York: Macmillan Company, 1966), p. 160.

[6] Yves Congar, *Dialogue Between Christians* (London: Geoffrey Chapman Limited, 1966; Paramus, N. J.: Paulist/Newman Press, 1967).

[7] Arthur A. Vogel, *Is the Last Supper Finished: Sacred Light on a Sacred Meal* (New York: Sheed & Ward, Inc., 1968), p. 64.

[8] Ibid., pps. 39, 160, 25, 26. Cf Teilhard de Chardin, *The Divine Milieu* (New York: Harper & Row, Publishers, 1960), pp. 125-126. "The eucharistic transformation goes beyond and completes the consecration of the heart on the altar. Step by step it irresistibly invades the universe. It is the fire that sweeps the heath."

[9] Nathan A. Scott, *The Wild Prayer of Longing: Poetry and the Sacred* (New Haven, Conn.: Yale University Press, 1971), p. xiv.

[10] Ibid., pp. 117-118.

[11] F. D. Maurice, *The Gospel of John* (London: Macmil-

Ian Company, 1888), p. 66.

[12] Ibid., p. 264.

[13] Metropolitan Anthony Bloom, *Meditations On a Theme* (London: A. R. Mowbray & Co., Ltd., 1972), pp. 7-8.

[14] Archimandrite Sofrony, *The Undistorted Image, Staretz Silouan, 1866-1938* (London: Faith Press, 1958), p. 173. This book is now out of print. A new edition is planned in the *Cistercian Fathers Series* directed from the monastery at Spencer, Massachusetts.

[15] Ibid., p. 189.

[16] Ibid., p. 70.

[17] Ibid., p. 150.

[18] The best introduction to the practice of the Jesus Prayer is to be found in a small book called *On the Invocation of the Name of Jesus* by a monk of the Eastern Church (Fellowship of St. Alban and St. Sergius, 52 Ladbroke Grove, London W.11.), though it is to be noted that the writer advises the use of the single word "Jesus," a practice not favored, at least at the beginning, by most spiritual teachers. *The Way of the Pilgrim* (translated by R. M. French, published by S.P.C.K., London) also gives a good and vivid account of the use of the Jesus Prayer.

"Did the letter writer call you?" I asked.

"Not yet," said Ms. Bases. "I'll hang up. I've got nothing to hide." She looked at the shadow painting of herself on the wall. "It's a pity. This ruins my feelings about the painting. I loved it, but now it looks dirty to me. I can't stand looking at it when I think of the lousy creep who must have painted it."

"Can I keep your letter for a while?" I asked. "Diana and I are going to catch the lousy creep."

"Sure, you'll save me the trouble of burning it." I put Ms. Bases' note in my pocket along with my own. Some detective I was turning out to be. It was one thing to tell Ms. Bases we were going to catch the creep. All I had so far was a big fat zero.

"Where to next?" Diana asked.

I consulted my map.

"The Don't Go Down Lady."

"Oh no," groaned Diana.

"We've got to check them all out," I said.

The Don't Go Down Lady was on her corner by the subway entrance. Her shopping cart was by her side. "Hello," I said. "It was good to see you at the meeting."

"Don't go down," she answered. Her eyes looked more cloudy than usual.

"This is my sister, Diana."

She gave Diana a sideways glance. "Don't go down," she hissed.

I felt sad that she was back to saying nothing but "don't go down."

"Did you get a threatening letter?" I asked.

"DON'T GO DOWN!" she shouted.

I jumped. Diana ducked behind me.

"Don't worry," I said. "I'm going to catch the twerp who did the paintings and wrote the letter." I was sure that she had gotten a letter too.

Diana gave her a backwards glance as we left the subway stop in a hurry. "I told you we shouldn't have bothered with her," said Diana. "She's nuts."

"She isn't," I said. "When she came to the meeting, she could talk in sentences. She's just scared of something."

"Why would anyone blackmail her?" Diana asked. "She has even less money than you do."

"You're right," I said. "It doesn't make sense. It looks like the blackmailer is sending letters to everyone whose shadow was painted. It doesn't seem to matter who they are."

"Why not just do pictures of rich people?" asked Diana. "At least if you blackmail a rich person, there's a chance you'll get paid."

"You know," I said thoughtfully, "that's a very good question."

A Nose Job

It was still pretty early for a basketball game. On a Saturday morning, most of the players don't even wake up until noon. But Wily Will was on the court, warming up with some shadow boxing. Diana and I watched him from outside the chain link fence. His hands were fast, punching the air, pow, pow, pow.

I looked down at his shadow painting. Something bothered me about that shadow. I opened my notebook and looked down at the sketch I had made of Wily Will during the meeting.

"Look at his nose," I whispered to Diana.

"It's rude to stare."

"I mean at the nose of his shadow painting," I said.

Just then Wily Will stopped shadow boxing and came over to the fence, dribbling the basket-

ball. "That your girlfriend, Lamont? You rob-
bing the cradle?"

I blushed.

"I'm Lamont's sister, Diana. I'm named after
Wonder Woman."

"Wonder Woman, huh?" Wily Will sniffed.

"I call her Wonder Shrimp," I said.

"Wonder Woman was the greatest Amazon of
all!" shouted Diana.

"You play basketball, Amazon?"

Diana and I went out on the court. "Hey, Wily
Will, Diana doesn't have any money."

"I don't hustle little kids. Come on, I'll give
you a few pointers." He flung the ball at Diana.
"Shoot," he said.

She tried to make a lay-up and missed.

"Try again," said Wily Will. He bounced the
ball to her.

Diana missed again.

Wily Will gave me the ball. I made my first
jump shot.

Wily Will grinned at me. "Not bad for a
shadow."

"Let me try again," said Diana.

Diana tried. She came close, but she missed
again. "Stop looking at the ground so much,"
Wily Will advised.

"I can't help it," said Diana. "The shadow on

the court looks so much like you, except . . . ."

"Diana!" I shouted. "Be careful . . . uh . . . careful of where you shoot," I added quickly.

I looked down at the shadow painting. My guess was right. The artist hadn't made a mistake on any of the other paintings.

Diana made a basket. She whooped with joy. Wily Will winked at me. "Your sister's not Wonder Woman, but she's . . . ."

I stared at Wily Will's nose. I wanted to be wrong.

"What are you staring at kid?" Wily Will asked.

There was only one thing I could say. "The Shadow Nose."

"You're talking crazy," said Wily Will, but he rubbed his broken nose, and I knew that I was right.

"You're the shadow artist," I said. "Every other shadow painting was absolutely accurate, down to the bump on my nose, Zylber's fat belly, Ms. Bases' stringy legs. None of the rest of us were prettied up. But you gave yourself a nose job."

Wily Will threw the ball back at me. I stumbled back on Diana, and we both fell right on Wily Will's shadow. Wily Will under us, Wily

Will above us, we were surrounded. He glared as if he was ready to turn us into permanent shadows.

"You think you can pick up that hundred dollars on a nose," snarled Wily Will.

I picked myself up off the ground. "This painting of you is really my favorite," I said. "That way it shows you going up for a jump shot. It's the most beautiful one of them all."

"Thanks," muttered Wily Will. His hand jumped to his mouth.

"You're welcome," I said. "You're a great artist and a rotten human being."

I dusted myself off. Wily Will grabbed me by the collar. "What did you say?" His face was just inches from mine.

"You're choking me," I squawked.

Diana jumped on Wily Will's back. She clung to him like a shadow. Finally Wily Will let me go and Diana scrambled off his back. "You made those shadow paintings just to scare people," Diana shouted angrily.

"What's the chick talking about?" Wily Will asked me.

"Watch who you call a chick," warned Diana. "I'll turn you into a scrambled egg."

"Can't you shut her up?"

I shook my head. "Nobody can, but she's right anyhow. You must have sent the letters to everyone. You must have figured that everyone has a secret in their past that they want to hide."

"I'm telling you Lamont, I don't know what you're talking about."

Wily Will's eyes wouldn't let me go. I didn't know what to believe. Wily Will was a hustler on the basketball court, true. But somehow I didn't believe he was a bad guy.

I took the letters out of my pocket and showed them to him.

"What are you doing?" demanded Diana. "We need those letters for evidence. We've got to take them to the P–O–L–I–C–E."

"I know how to spell, girlie."

Diana started to open her mouth, but something about Wily Will's expression made her close it again. Will crushed one letter in his hand. "Where did you get this?"

"It was on top of our mailbox this morning. It wasn't sent through the mails."

"You wrote those letters," said Diana. "You're the shadow artist."

I shook my head. "I don't think you wrote them, Wily Will. I think you did the paintings, but you didn't write the letters."

"You're crazy, Lamont," said Diana. "He's got you conned."

"Look at the shadow paintings," I said, pointing down to the beautiful painting of Wily Will on the court. "They're perfect. Do you think the same person who did the paintings on the sidewalks would make those splotches on the letters?"

Wily Will bounced the ball up and down on his painted shadow. "You're right, Lamont. I did the paintings on the street, but I never sent *anybody* any letters. I wouldn't have done that. I only painted people I liked. I've always loved to draw, all my life, but I never thought I could make any money at it. I dropped out of school. I can't get a job, so I hustle basketball games. But no crime. I've stayed clean. Then one day, I caught sight of my shadow when I was going for a lay-up. It looked beautiful to me. I started painting shadows on the street. It was my secret life. But I don't *blackmail!*"

"But if you didn't send the letters, who did?" Diana asked.

"That's what we've got to find out," I said.

P·O·L·I·S·E

"Thanks." Wily Will put his big hands on my shoulders. "Thanks for believing me."

"Forget it," I said. "Just because I believe you, doesn't mean you're in the clear. Does anybody else know you're the shadow artist?"

Wily Will shook his head. "No. I made sketches of the paintings, but I kept them hidden in my room at the YMCA, the one I share with Swivel Hips. I've always been quick with my hands, in paintings just like in basketball. I do the paintings *real* fast."

Just then Swivel Hips George came onto the court. "Hey, Wily Will, you playing with girl shadows now?" he asked.

"I'm not a shadow," snapped Diana.

"Hey, be cool, George," said Wily Will. "These kids here are my friends."

I felt proud that Wily Will would call me his friend. Swivel Hips George didn't seem to like it. He gave Diana and me a dirty look. "Hand me that ball," he said.

Diana dribbled the ball in front of her. She made no move to pass it.

"Did you hear me?" asked Swivel Hips.

Suddenly I had an idea. "Hey, Swivel Hips," I said. "I bet Wily Will that he couldn't spell police, and I won five dollars."

"You won five dollars off Wily Will? A little pipsqueak like you?"

Wily Will spread out his huge hands. He shrugged. "The kid made a bet and he won."

"Ha," snorted Swivel Hips.

"I'll give you a chance to win it back for Wily Will. I'll bet you ten bucks you can't spell police."

"Ha. I can spell police. I can *smell* police. I just don't *like* police. Ten bucks isn't enough."

"Twenty bucks says you can't." My stomach was doing somersaults. I had twenty dollars in my pocket, but it was the money Mom and Dad gave me to do the weekend food shopping. If I lost it, I would be in big, big trouble.

Swivel Hips stopped dribbling. "What's the con, kid? You think I'm stupid or something?"

"I just don't think you can spell police."

Swivel Hips George swiveled away. He made a lay-up. "Kid, I'm not going to bite."

"Okay," I said. "I'll give you odds. Ten to one."

"Ha, it's a sucker bet."

"Look, I'll make it twenty to one."

"Lamont," said Diana. "Can I talk to you?" She grabbed my arm and half dragged me over to the fence. "Lamont, are you crazy? Even I know that's a stupid bet. Do you know that means you have to pay four hundred dollars if you lose? Four hundred dollars! What are you going to do?"

"I'm not going to lose," I said.

Wily Will came over to us. "Lamont, do you know what you're doing?"

"I'm on a roll," I said.

Wily Will and Diana exchanged anxious glances. "If you ask me," said Diana, "he's gone bonkers."

"Easiest bucks I'll ever earn," sneered Swivel Hips. "P–O–L. . . ."

I held my breath. If I was wrong, I was sunk deeper than the Titanic. I looked across the street and my stomach did a triple somersault. A police car was parked right in front of the playground. The word POLICE was there in big blue letters. All Swivel Hips had to do was look across

the street, and all that money would fly away.

Diana followed my eyes. Casually she skipped to the far side of the playground, away from the street. Swivel Hips kept his eyes on her. "That girl is ruining my concentration," he said.

"Diana, stand still," I ordered, thankful she'd been smart enough to keep Swivel Hips from looking at the police car.

"Go on, Swivel Hips," said Wily Will. "Finish the word."

"P–O–L–I–S–E."

"Just like you spelled it on the blackmail notes you've been writing!" I shouted.

"Ha," snorted Swivel Hips. "Since when is it a crime to misspell a word? You gonna call the police?"

"We just might do that," I said. "Blackmail is against the law."

Wily Will glowered at Swivel Hips. "You sent those stupid letters to everyone except *me* cause you knew I'd recognize your handwriting."

"You recognized his handwriting?" I asked.

Wily Will nodded. "As soon as I saw it. You don't think I'd have let you really risk four hundred dollars."

"I was scared," I admitted. But I realized that you were the only one who didn't get a note. It had to be Swivel Hips. Since you were room-mates, he knew you'd guess he was sending the notes."

"Now, wait a minute, Will," Swivel Hips pleaded. "No need to get all hot and bothered. I would have given you a cut. Seeing those shadows made me think. I figured everyone had something to hide. Then, when you said Lamont was The Shadow, I got a great idea. I just dropped off my little notes after you did the paintings. I figured the kid would be blamed."

Wily Will looked as if he wanted to kill Swivel Hips. "You lousy creep. I liked those people I drew. I only joked about Lamont's name because I didn't want anyone to guess it was me. Now you've ruined everything." He lunged for Swivel Hips.

"Hold it, Wily Will," I said.

"Right," said Diana, running over to the police car. "Help!" she shouted. "P–O–L–I–C–E!"

The Real Nose

We all went to the police station. It was a mad-house. The police, of course, knew all about the shadow paintings. They even knew about the blackmail. Mr. Zylber had taken his note to them. But it took them a long time to understand that there were two shadows. The artist and the creep!

The police called all the people who had received notes and asked them to come to the station. They also called my mom and dad.

Swivel Hips called a lawyer.

"Some friend," snorted Wily Will as he watched Swivel Hips make his phone call. We were sitting on a bench in the precinct house. Wily Will was slumped on the bench. He looked more sad than mad.

"I'm sorry it turned out to be your friend," I said.

"He's no friend," said Wily Will. "And don't waste your time feeling sorry about Swivel Hips. He probably won't stay in jail very long, if at all."

"It's not Swivel Hips I'm worried about," I said. "It's you."

"Yeah, what about you, Wily Will?" asked Diana. "What are you going to do now?"

Wily Will shrugged. "I guess I'll go back to the playground and hustle up a game." Wily Will rubbed his nose. "To think, all because of a nose. I was just too vain to paint my nose the way it is. Well, you taught me a lesson, Lamont. I'm going to keep my paintings in a deep shadow from now on. . . ."

I was mad. Wily Will's talent was too good to stay in a closet.

Just then my parents came bursting into the precinct house.

"Lamont!" cried my mother. "What's wrong?"

"Nothing. Calm down. I found out who the shadow artist is," I said.

"In the police station?" asked my father.

"No, on the basketball court. Mom and Dad,

I want you to meet the best artist on the street, Will . . ." I paused. I realized I never knew Wily Will's last name.

"Will Harris," mumbled Wily Will.

My father held out his hand. "Pleased to meet you Will. I've been admiring your art every time I leave my front door. It sort of stares me in the face. You've got a lot of talent."

"And Dad's a professional artist," said Diana proudly.

Wily Will looked embarrassed.

"Who's the artist?" demanded Ms. Bases. She was followed by Mr. Zylber. The Don't Go Down Lady stood shyly in the corner.

"I'm no artist," said Wily Will softly.

I introduced Wily Will to everybody. The police had already explained to them that the blackmail letters had not come from the shadow artist and that the blackmailer was in custody.

"You!" said Ms. Bases. "I've seen you on the basketball court. What are you wasting your time playing basketball for?"

"Good question," said my father.

Wily Will looked as if he wanted to disappear.

"Hey," piped up Diana. "We win the reward! We found the shadow artist."

"That's right," said my mother. "Lamont, I guess you and Diana have won the reward."

"I won it," I argued. "I won it by a nose."

Diana squinched up her face. "But I helped."

I sighed. "You did," I admitted. I looked over in the corner. My father was in deep conversation with Wily Will. I wondered what they were talking about.

"Diana, I've got an idea," I said.

"Oh no," warned Diana. "Your ideas usually end up getting us in trouble."

"This one won't," I promised. "It's a great way we can share the reward."

"I already know a great way. You get fifty bucks, and I get fifty bucks."

"No, this is better." I whispered my idea in Diana's ear.

At first she didn't like it, but the more she heard, the better it sounded to her. Finally, she nodded her head. "Okay," she whispered back. "But we share it, remember."

I agreed.

"What's up?" asked my mom.

I cleared my throat. "I have an announcement," I said. "As you know, Diana and I have just won a hundred dollars. We want to buy a painting. In fact, we want your painting, Wily Will. We would like you to put our favorite shadow painting on canvas, the one of you going for a lay-up."

"Right," said Diana. "Because, I'm going to grow up to be a great basketball player, and your painting will inspire me."

For a wonder shrimp, Diana's got great dreams.

Wily Will stared at us. "You'd pay a hundred dollars just for a painting?"

My father smiled. "That's what I was talking to you about. Actually I think Lamont and Diana are making a good investment. If you have the guts to stick with painting, I think you could go far. You sure have the raw talent for it."

Ms. Bases practically sprang forward. "I have to admit that your shadow paintings have attracted a number of tourists. I have a feeling that if I carried some of your paintings in my shop, I might be able to sell them. We'll have to talk about commissions, of course."

Wily Will smiled. He and Ms. Bases had a lot in common. They both liked a good hustle.

The Don't Go Down Lady motioned to me. She whispered in my ear.

"Wily Will," I said. "This lady would like you to sign her painting by the subway entrance."

Wily Will nodded gravely. "I'd be glad to," he said.

"But our painting should come first," said Diana. "We asked first."

"And we want you to correct the nose," I
added. "We want the real Wily Will's nose."

"Right," said Wily Will. He laughed. I had
never seen Wily Will look so happy. "Well, it
looks like I might not be having too much time
for basketball these days."

My father put his arm around Will's shoulder.
"Why don't you come around to my studio and
we'll have a long talk."

"Thanks," said Will. "I'd like it."

We walked out of the precinct house. Dad and Will were deep in conversation. Mom was talking to Ms. Bases. Diana and I trailed behind.

"It's weird," she said.

"What's weird?" I asked.

"We just caught a creepy blackmailer and already everyone has forgotten about him. All anybody cares about is Wily Will and his art."

"It seems right," I said. "There will always be lots of creeps like Swivel Hips around, but there aren't many Wily Wills in the world."

"There aren't many Lamont Shapiros in the world either," said Diana. "Where would the shadow artist be without the original Shadow!" She flashed me a smile.

For a wonder shrimp, Diana isn't all bad. In fact, sometimes she lives up to her name. Sometimes I do too. We make a good pair.